A Social Gospel For Millions

A Social Gospel For Millions:

The Religious Bestsellers of Charles Sheldon, Charles Gordon, and Harold Bell Wright

John P. Ferré

Bowling Green State University Popular Press
Bowling Green, Ohio 43403

Cover design by Gary Dumm and Greg Budgett

Contents

Acknowledgments

My interest in bestselling religious books began at Mars Hill College where I analyzed *In His Steps* for an American culture paper I wrote for Joseph Schubert. My interest in the social gospel grew when I studied theological modernism with Larry Greenfield at the University of Chicago. I combined these two concerns at the University of Illinois, first in a popular culture course I took from Clifford Christians, then in the dissertation I wrote for Cliff and for James Carey and Willard Rowland. I am grateful to all of them for their guidance and criticism.

I also owe thanks to Gweneth Dunleavy, my wife, who suggested alternative ways of understanding these texts, and to Leon Driskill of the University of Louisville, who critiqued the entire manuscript.

Chapter One

Social Gospel Bestsellers

Charles Sheldon, Charles Gordon, and Harold Bell Wright were the bestselling religious writers during the late nineteenth and early twentieth centuries, the time known alternatively as the social gospel period or the Third Great Awakening in the United States. Both the social gospel, associated with the thinkers Washington Gladden, Richard T. Ely, and Walter Rauschenbusch, and the Third Great Awakening, associated with the evangelists Reuben A. Torrey, Billy Sunday, and Dwight L. Moody, were religious responses to myriad upheavals in economics, psychology, and biology, and in industry, technology, and demographics. Marx was prophesying the end of western capitalism by means of the workers who suffered systematic exploitation; Freud was explaining human behavior in terms of infantile sexuality and the unconscious; and Darwin was convincing scientists that all animals, including human beings, were the result of selective adaptation to the environment rather than of any purposeful creative design.

These challenges to orthodoxy form a backdrop to the religious novels of Sheldon, Gordon, and Wright, novels that outsold almost every other novel of the era. Understanding these bestsellers is important historically because they indicate how the middle class responded to the intellectual and material changes that confronted them. This understanding also has broad conceptual importance because it can illuminate the relationship between mass-mediated messages and a culture's value system. For historical and conceptual purposes, then, the religious bestsellers of Sheldon, Gordon, and Wright require examination.

Change
As Marx, Freud, and Darwin were leading intellectual changes,

1

a host of material changes were also occurring. Between 1889 and 1919, industrial productivity increased one per cent per year, the result of technological innovations rather than human workers (Conn 1983, 7). Industry became wealthier and increasingly centralized. In 1901, for instance, U.S. Steel capitalized $1.4 billion, three times what the United States government spent in a year (Conn 1983, 10). Emery reports that "in 1914 one-eighth of American businesses employed more than three-fourths of the wage earners and produced four-fifths of the manufactured products" (1972, 381).

The increasing power of industry elicited strong reactions by government and labor. The federal government moved further and further away from its policy of laissez-faire, passing the Interstate Commerce Act in 1887 and the Sherman Anti-Trust Act in 1890. Labor organized steadily. The most powerful national labor coalition, the American Federation of Labor, began in Columbus, Ohio late in 1886 with 250 thousand members; by 1904, the A.F. of L. had 1,676,000 paid members (Mowry 1958, 10). The grossly underpaid laborers, frustrated by the wealth of their employers, grew increasingly violent. In the thirty-month period following January 1902, "180 union men were killed, 1,651 injured, and over 5,000 arrested" (Mowry 1958, 11).

Perhaps the crowning industrial achievement of this age was the automobile, and the assembly line that was the key to its mass production. Henry Ford, with outside capital that he had attracted with a race car that he built in 1902, began the Ford Motor Company in 1903. Five years later, he introduced the Model T, an inexpensive, compact car with a high chassis that was well suited to the horse and wagon roads of the time. Within a year of its introduction, Ford had sold ten thousand Model Ts. To meet the heavy demand, Ford used assembly-line techniques to cut the manufacturing time of a car from twelve hours and twenty-eight minutes in 1913 to ninety-three minutes at the end of 1914. The workers' monotony and turnover increased with the rate of production, so Ford compensated by paying a record five dollars a day. Between 1914 and 1916, Ford Motor Company's turnover dropped ninety per cent and its profits doubled to $60 million after taxes (Noble 1970, 39-40). Some eight thousand automobiles traveled on 150 miles of pavement in 1900; fifteen years later, some two and a half million automobiles traveled on thousands of miles of pavement. "What had been a novelty," writes Peter Conn, "had become one of the principal technical and sociological phenomena of the twentieth century" (1983, 7).

Technological innovation coincided with population growth and demographic change. Between 1898 and 1917, the population of the United States grew from 75 million to 100 million, largely because of immigration. This statistic is striking given that the population of the United States at the close of the Civil War was a mere thirty million. In 1910, one out of every seven Americans was foreign born. These immigrants differed greatly from their predecessors. Most came from southern and eastern Europe—from Italy, Austria-Hungary, Poland, and Russia—not from northern and western Europe. They were Roman Catholic or Jewish, not Protestant. Often poor and illiterate, many of them immigrated in order to make enough money to put them in good stead in their homelands, not to settle permanently in the United States.

The immigrants were settling in large numbers in the rapidly growing cities. Sixty per cent of Americans lived either on farms or in towns of fewer than 2500 people in 1900, but by 1920 more than half of the population lived in urban areas. This demographic change worried a great number of people, particularly in the agricultural South and Midwest, who believed that the country's change from a rural, agricultural economy to an urban, industrial one signaled the decline of cultural purity and the rise of cultural decadence. The culture was becoming artificial, unnatural. William Jennings Bryan's "Cross of Gold" speech at the 1896 Democratic Convention epitomizes this feeling:

Bryan defined his role as a defender of rural innocence against the aggressive, rapacious finance capitalists of the urban East. His listeners knew that Bryan was attempting to defend sacred Americanism against profane un-Americanism, to defend productive yeomen against parasitical aliens. In their innocence these true American people had retreated from their attackers until their backs were against the abyss and they could retreat no more. At such a moment the innocents must fight to preserve their virtue (Noble 1970, 13).

George Mowry observed that the first two decades of the twentieth century witnessed the sharpest division between urban and rural American in the country's history (1958, 14). This city-country division was essentially a clash between the value systems of the new immigrants and the old, Catholics and Jews and Protestants, and manufacturing and farming.

Nothing short of revolutionary, these changes profoundly challenged the conservatism of the Protestant churches in America. When asked to rank religious groups according to their friendliness towards labor, Samuel Gompers, longtime president of the A.F. of L., listed Protestants and ministers last after ethical societies, Unitarians, nonbelievers, and Catholics. Similarly, a poll taken in 1900 revealed that workers did not attend church because they perceived Protestantism as an instrument of the capitalist rich which condemned labor unions and strikes (Mowry 1958, 25). Protestantism responded to the intellectual and material upheavals, and to its growing disfavor, with the social gospel and with evangelical revivals.

Response

The revivals were a conservative response to the revolutions in thought and experience that the country was undergoing. Reuben A. Torrey, Billy Sunday, and Dwight L. Moody may have preached about social issues, but except for favoring what became the Eighteenth Amendment to the Constitution, Prohibition of the demon alcohol, they found solace in the converted thoughts and actions of the individual rather than in social or political action. They preached the salvation of individual souls, using their interpretations of the Bible as their authority. They thought that theories threatened the plain truth of the Bible and that labor movements distracted attention from the work of spreading the gospel. According to William McLoughlin,

Moody's revivals in the 1870's were the opening and half-unconscious battle of the modernist-fundamentalist schism. Theistic evolution, progressive orthodoxy, 'the new theology,' and the higher criticism were significant elements in the same reorientation. By 1915, the modernists were assuming control of the denominations and the seminaries while the fundamentalists rallied around the revivalism of Billy Sunday. The ecclesiastical fireworks of the 1920's...were pure anticlimax (1959, 10).

Moody's revivals highlight the strong individualism of Protestant piety during this period. The gospel that Moody preached concerned God's saving grace which could be experienced through repentance. Such an experience would cause the converted individual to live morally. Public morality would improve only to the extent that great numbers of individuals were truly converted. Morality was understood to be individual; it became public only because there are millions of individuals. According to Moody, any public act of charity was a way to attract a candidate for conversion; society would improve only if more individuals were converted (Ahlstrom 1972, 203).

Just as business was becoming large and centralized, Moody adapted evangelism to a centralized business model that evangelists like Billy Graham still use today. Moody entered full-time evangelism after he had become a successful shoe salesman in Chicago and had worked intimately with the Y.M.C.A. there. Because large cities provided an efficient setting for winning souls, Moody led city-wide revivals in New York, Philadelphia, Boston, Chicago, Baltimore, St. Louis, Cleveland, and San Francisco. In these cities, his work was a choice example of marketing efficiency, as Winthrop Hudson points out:

Everything was carefully planned in advance. There were committees for finance, prayer, publicity, home visitation, Bible study, music, tickets, and ushering. An executive committee was appointed to make sure that all the other committees functioned properly. No advertising device was neglected, and considerable sums were spent on posters and newspaper notices.... Cities were divided into districts, and squads of workers were trained and sent out to visit each home (1973, 232).

Moody's efficiency in disseminating his gospel of individualism made for a potent reactionary force in the face of the period's intellectual and material turmoil.

The reactions to modernism by the revivalists led to the entrenchment of fundamentalism beginning with the Niagara Conference of 1876, which eventually produced the five shibboleths of fundamentalist Christianity: the verbal and inerrant inspiration of the Bible, the virgin birth, substitutionary atonement, bodily resurrection, and the imminent second coming of Jesus Christ. The reactions of the evangelical revivalists support Conn's thesis that "the accelerating shocks of the future were met by the redoubled claims of the past" (1983, 13). Carlos Baker put this argument in a religious context when he said that "in times of social stress in the United States there has been a tendency to turn back for ethical ideals and values to ancient religious literature" (Smith and Jamison

1961, 266). This argument is particularly poignant given that Protestant churches were growing faster than the country's population, to some extent because of the successful fervor of the revivalists, even as the swelling ranks of labor were growing increasingly critical of Protestantism (Handy 1966, 3).

Protestants did not meet these changes with conservatism or nostalgia alone, however. Some Protestant clergymen began to feel that the long-standing focus on individual salvation by revivalists like Dwight L. Moody ignored the realities of urban social life. Those dissatisfied with the individualism of the revivals began to preach what became known as the social gospel, a rejection of Adam Smith's philosophy of laissez-faire and Spencer's social Darwinism in favor of Christian ethics applied to institutional issues.

The social gospel movement, which rose to a peak between the turn of the century and World War I, was composed of three broad divisions. One was conservative. It recognized social problems but advocated few structural or institutional changes, relying instead upon individual moral enlightenment for changes in the marketplace. Conservative advocates of the social gospel, like the Boston ministers Joseph Cook and Minot J. Savage, did favor laws regulating the hours, pay, and working conditions of women and children in the factories, but their arguments were more prudent than revolutionary. By voluntarily paying higher wages, they said, factory owners would minimize clashes with labor.

At the other extreme were the Christian socialists such as W. D. P. Bliss and George D. Herron who believed that the only way to christianize the social order was to replace democratic capitalism with socialism. Bliss, an Episcopal priest, organized the Society of Christian Socialists in Boston in 1889. He left the parish ministry in 1890 to found the Mission of the Carpenter in Boston which published a newspaper called *The Dawn*. By 1906 Bliss was an active member of the Socialist party. Similarly Herron, who taught Applied Christianity at Grinnell College, was so integral to the Socialist party that he was chosen to give the nominating speech for Eugene Debs at the party's 1904 Chicago convention.

Between the conservatives like Cook and Savage and the radicals like Bliss and Herron were such centrist figures as Washington Gladden (the so-called father of the social gospel), Richard T. Ely, and Walter Rauschenbusch. They emphasized the immanence of God in human affairs, the relevance of Christian love to the economy, and the increase of beneficence in social relations. Using the First Congregational Church in Columbus, Ohio as his home base, Gladden wrote some thirty books in which he advocated the organization of labor, maximum-hours laws, factory inspection, and federal regulation of natural monopolies (Boller 1969, 121). Ely, a professor at Johns Hopkins, belonged to what he called "the ethical school of economists." His widely-read *Social Aspects of Christianity* (1889) related culture, religion, and ethics to economics. Liberal social gospellers, particularly Walter Rauschenbusch, were not content with superficial reforms of certain capitalist practices. They rejected the socialist option, but strenuously argued for a Christian cooperative order to replace capitalism.

The most articulate social gospel advocate was Rauschenbusch, who spent ten years as a Baptist minister in Hell's Kitchen in New York before joining the faculty of Rochester Theological Seminary. Like other proponents of the social gospel, he emphasized the Kingdom of God, a biblical symbol he interpreted to mean that God reigns over the social order just as he reigns over individuals. In his three major books, *Christianity and the Social Crisis* (1907), *Christianizing the Social Order* (1912), and *A Theology for the Social Gospel* (1917), Rauschenbusch argued that the entire social gospel can be understood in the idea of the Kingdom of God, which he explicitly tied to Darwin's theory of evolution:

Translate the evolutionary theories into religious faith, and you have the doctrine of the kingdom of God. This combination with scientific evolutionary thought has freed the kingdom ideal of its catastrophic setting and its background of demonism, and so adapted it to the climate of the modern world (1912, 90).

To speak of the Kingdom, which is in a constant process of evolution, is to speak of the perpetually improving social order. But sin, as much a social force as an individual one, retards the Kingdom's realization. In *A Theology for the Social Gospel*, Rauschenbusch wrote, "We rebel against God and repudiate his will when we set our profit and ambition above the welfare of our fellows and above the Kingdom of God which binds them together" (1917, 48).

Rauschenbusch believed that four of five social orders in the United States had already been christianized. The family, religion, education, and politics had passed through despotism and exploitation and become primarily democratic. But because business was ruled by capitalism, it was unregenerate and it threatened to undermine the successful christianization of the other orders. Business was at the core of social problems, Rauschenbusch wrote, because it squandered humanity for the love of money. By relegating wealth to a few, capitalism contradicted the spirit of Christ, causing injustice, inequality, and a two-class system. Business was in sore need of Christian conversion:

The fundamental step of repentance and conversion for professions and organizations is to give up monopoly power and the incomes derived from legalized extortion, and to come under the law of service, content with a fair income from honest work. The corresponding step in the case of governments and political oligarchies, semi-democracies, is to submit to real democracy. Therewith they step out of the Kingdom of Evil into the Kingdom of God (1917, 117).

Rauschenbusch, Gladden, and Ely were prolific, but their books were restricted to a fairly esoteric readership. Although their ideas were also proclaimed from Protestant pulpits and reported in the popular press, the social gospel would have been much more contained were it not for the steady production of social gospel novels. Between 1886 and 1914, three or four social gospel novels were published per year (Nicholl 1964, 1-2). Their appeal had much to do with the social and economic unrest as well as the questioning of orthodoxy at the time (Hart 1954, 320).

Besides being informed by the social gospel movement in American Protestantism, these novels descended from certain literary influences. One was the religious motifs in pre-Civil War novels, such as in Harriet Beecher Stowe's *Uncle Tom's Cabin*, which she contended was the result of divine dictation. A second influence was the genteel romance to which religious themes were added. Publications like *Godey's Ladies' Books, Scribner's Monthly*, and the *Atlantic Monthly* were full of love stories with happy endings. Many of the Christian social novels were love stories that took place in the midst of social reform. A third influence was the impact of two British novels: Mrs. Humphrey Ward's *Robert Elsmere* (1888) and Hall Caine's *The Christian* (1897). The protagonist in each book is a minister who doubts the orthodox faith, leaves the parish, converts to liberalism, and finally finds fulfillment doing social work in the slums of London. American social gospel novelists were also highly influenced by another British novel, *If Christ Came to Chicago!* (1894), written by William T. Stead after a visit to the city. The novel asks what Christ would want readers to do after he witnessed the economic exploitation, political corruption, alcohol consumption, and crime in the city—particularly given the churches' apparent indifference. Other If-Christ-Came novels followed shortly thereafter: Milford W. Howard's *If Christ Came to Congress* (1894), Isaac G. Reed, Jr.'s *From Heaven to New York* (1894), Edward E. Hale's *If Jesus Came to Boston* (1895), Olla P. Toph's *Lazarus* (1895), Elizabeth Phelps Ward's *The Supply at Saint Agatha's* (1896), and Cortland Myers' *Would Christ Belong to a Labor Union?* (1900) (Nicholl 1964, 7-25).

During the era of the social gospel novel, the reading of fiction became a national pastime: "Novels were devoured as much as read, and the public appetite appeared to be insatiable. Advertising budgets reflected this phenomenon; most houses used about 70 per cent of them for fiction" (Tebbel 1975, 170). The rising interest in novels was partially due to the increase of compulsory education, the increase in high school and college enrollment, and the spread of the library movement (encouraged by funding from Andrew Carnegie). Such educational movements helped to spawn numerous literary societies which met regularly to study literature and the arts (Mott 1947, 183-84). The large sales of novels were buoyed by the net pricing system adopted nationally shortly after the turn of the century, which standardized the margin of profit that publishers and booksellers made on each book they sold—as well as by the growing number of department store book departments and the increasing popularity of fiction magazines (Tebbel 1975, 174).

By 1897, when Charles Sheldon's *In His Steps* was published, religious publishers understood that books with popular appeal would sell widely if they were promoted and sold in inexpensive editions. For the popular appeal, publishers located fiction that responded to the social and intellectual upheavals both within and outside the churches. Disregarding the Bible and collections of Bible stories and verses, novels by Charles Sheldon, Charles Gordon, and Harold Bell Wright were the only religious books published between 1897 and World War I which sold to one per cent of the population (Mott 1947, 303). *In His Steps* (1897, Advance) by Charles M. Sheldon sold eight million copies, *Black Rock* (1898, Fleming H. Revell) by "Ralph Connor," pseudonym for Charles Gordon, sold well over half a million copies, and *The Shepherd of the Hills* (1907,

Book Supply) and *The Calling of Dan Matthews* (1909, Book
Supply) by Harold Bell Wright sold 1.2 million and 925,000 copies
respectively. These were the religious bestsellers of the social gospel
era.

Interpretation

Interpreting the cultural meaning of religious bestsellers
requires a symbolic theory of the relationship between mass media
messages and culture. According to this approach, cultural symbols
and myths form a web of meaning and feeling that both reflects
the way that a culture perceives and values reality as well as shapes
the perceptions and motivations of those who share the myth and
symbol system. John Cawelti recently reiterated this approach: "The
idea that the media reflect, express and probably reinforce attitudes
and values is a more subtle, flexible and, in my opinion, more
fruitful application of the assumption that the media are involved
with values" (1985, 365-66).

Cawelti argues that literary formulas, not any particular element
within a story, link literature with society. He says that examining
"the dialectic between artistic formulas and cultural materials
should reveal something about the way in which people in a given
culture are predisposed to think about their lives" (1976, 31). Literary
formulas provide a sense of order and continuity, and the various
conflicts that arise within each formula story provide vicarious
adventure and excitement. Through literary formulas, the writer
and the readers share a "network of assumptions" which expresses
cultural values.

Cawelti offers four hypotheses concerning the relationship
between formulas and the culture which produces and uses them.
First, formulas present a structured experience of imagination that
affirms social values. Westerns, for instance, affirm the belief that
justice is individual rather than institutional. Second, formulas
harmonize conflicting values or ambivalences within a culture. In
the case of westerns, the individual's use of violence to protect the
community from anarchy harmonizes the anarchy of individualism
with the ideal of community. Third, formulas permit the audience
to indulge in taboos without sanctioning them. Again, westerns
allow the fantasy of lawlessness without condoning lawlessness in
practice. Finally, by assimilating changing values, formulas assist
in the value changes of the culture at large. Although westerns

have changed little, westerns now picture Indians as protectors of nature and home in contrast to their earlier role as savages (pp. 34-36).

The religious novels of Charles Sheldon, Charles Gordon, and Harold Bell Wright are melodramas, complex narratives that depict a world that appears to be violent and tragic, but which turns out to be governed by a benevolent morality. The stage for melodrama is a world which adheres to the audience's sense of good and evil. Melodramas typically contain a host of interwoven sub-plots, all based on an underlying moral principle, concerning the interconnected destinies of several individuals. The suffering that occurs in these stories serves as a test to demonstrate the soundness of the moral structure of the world. Melodramas sustain readers' interest by their rapid episodic intensity in which a character is dangled above a moral abyss; then they satisfy readers emotionally by ending happily. Because their moral code is bound tightly to the prevailing morality, melodramas are extraordinarily popular during their era, but they quickly become dated and thus appear arcane to succeeding generations. But in their time, melodramas can be socially powerful: "Because it directly implicates a world-view with particular social actions and characters, melodrama has the capacity for enormous social impact" (p. 46). *Uncle Tom's Cabin*, for instance, which presented black characters in the roles of Christian martyr, loving mother, and self-made hero, elicited strong reactions from Southern apologists who felt that Stowe's melodrama threatened their moral code.

Cawelti hints at the meaning of the popularity of Sheldon, Gordon, and Wright when he says that "the social melodrama seems to be the most time-bound of all the major formulas...because this formulaic type depends to such a great extent on the outlook and values of a particular era" (p. 263). Their novels employ melodramatic conventions, but they are what Cawelti calls bestselling *social* melodramas because they add a developed social setting to the emotionally satisfying melodrama: "The appeal of this synthesis combines the escapist satisfactions of melodrama— in particular, its fantasy of a moral universe following conventional social values—with the pleasurable feeling that we are learning something important about reality" (p. 261).

To argue that bestselling religious social melodramas share a network of social values with their readers is to beg the question of the role of advertising in the dissemination of these texts. If sales are primarily the result of advertising, the crucial text for analysis would be the advertisements, not the books. However, if John Harvey is correct, then the content of bestsellers is just as important as the publicity that they receive (1953, 91-114). Frederick Lewis Allen suggested that public acceptance of a book is influenced by the author's reputation, the publisher's confidence and marketing strategies, the reviewers' and booksellers' opinions, and book buyers' tendency to read what others are reading (1935, 3). Advertising does not neatly correlate with sales, as is clear from the experience at Zondervan Publishing House with the marketing of *The Late Great Planet Earth* by Hal Lindsay (1970), which has sold some ten million copies. According to Paul M. Hillman, Associate Publisher, "It was not expected to have great sales, only moderate sales. But we could not keep it in stock. It became the number one bestseller of all books, not just religious ones, in the 1970s" (1984). Books become bestsellers because a public wants to read them; advertising is only one element in the creation of public desire.

Although audience analyses are unavailable for the early twentieth century, contemporary studies of general book readers (Greene 1974) and religious book readers (Christian News Service 1975, 45-47), combined with a profile of religion in the United States at the turn of the century (Barrett 1982, 711), suggest who read the bestsellers of the social gospel period. Readers were more likely to be middle- and upper-class, suggesting persons who could afford to buy books; female, which would parallel church attendance patterns; high school educated, which would suggest mainline Protestantism; and young to middle-aged. The readers of religious bestsellers were middle class, and to the extent that they shared the network of myths and symbols of the books, this network of meaning belonged to the middle class. Grier Nicholl is probably near the truth in saying that "the recurring patterns of response found in [social gospel novels] represent the religious attitudes of millions of educated Protestants who read them, laymen inside the church, laymen outside the church who were still sympathetic to Christianity, and perhaps many ordinary ministers as well" (1964, 5).

Cawelti's argument that social melodramas reveal contemporary cultural values is a persuasive one—hence, the analysis of *In His Steps, Black Rock, The Shepherd of the Hills,* and *The Calling of Dan Matthews* as prime examples of religious social melodrama in the early twentieth century. But Cawelti does not provide a method for discerning the values within any given social melodrama. These titles deserve special scrutiny because they far outsold the other social melodramas of the time.

John Wiley Nelson asks five questions in order to discern the belief system of popular culture texts (1976). Because cultural phenomena that capture the public imagination affirm and support the culture's dominant belief (or value) system, Nelson identifies such phenomena as religious, calling popular culture "American cultural religion" (p. 19). To be an American, Nelson argues,

means to share values and beliefs about life and its meaning. These beliefs concern evil and its source, deliverance, and visions of the fulfilled and happy human life. In fact, "culture" is the manifestation of a system of shared beliefs about life's predicaments and solutions. There are potentially as many sets of beliefs as there are people, for no two people think exactly alike. But functioning societies in their most stable periods of self-understanding and expression produce a single dominant set of values which unifies all the shared individual or small-group beliefs into one characteristic belief system. At that point, to be an American means to affirm that dominant set of values (p. 19).

According to Nelson, a belief system is a systematic set of answers to questions regarding the optimum resolution of the problems of contemporary experience. To belong to a culture means to agree to the answers to the central life-problem questions, that is, to live according to the culture's belief system.

The first question of a culture's belief system concerns the *nature of evil.* Nelson suggests that, to Americans, evil is what prevents meaningful social relations or the maintenance of a desirable social institution. The second question concerns the *source of evil,* which Nelson says is invariably outside of the community. The third question concerns the source of deliverance, the *source of good.* Nelson suggests that in America, the source of good is always a self-sacrificing individual. The fourth issue is the *nature of the resolution.* Deliverance is for family and community life, according to Nelson. The final question concerns the *method for attaining resolution.* Nelson says that resolution of life problems according to the dominant American belief system is through mental and physical preparedness (pp. 20-25).

Put to the religious bestsellers in the early twentieth century, these questions can reveal the dominant religious belief system of the American middle-class. The answers illustrate the changes in commerce, technology, and law at the dawn of the twentieth century, but they do more than that. They also indicate moral responses to the changes that the country was undergoing at the time. The belief system of these social melodramas suggests that a significant portion of middle-class Americans in the early twentieth century responded to the turbulence of the times by romanticizing the frontier past, by emphasizing morality over belief, and by trusting individuals to solve the problems that they believed were created by social institutions.

Chapter Two

Charles Sheldon's Moral Formula

Social gospel novels were the legacy of the developments in American religious literature in general (Nicholl 1964, 2). From George Fowler's *The Wandering Philanthropist* (1810), to Susanna Rowson's *Biblical Dialogues Between a Father and his Family* (1822), to Elizabeth Phelps Ward's *The Gates Ajar* (1869), to Lew Wallace's *Ben-Hur* (1880), religious fiction countered the Puritan feeling that fiction, because it was not true, was frivolous if not subversive. Early religious fiction, which was biblicist and dogmatic, gave way to themes of toleration, moral perfectibility, and universal salvation (Reynolds 1981, 1-6). This development fit the tenor of nineteenth-century religious faith in America, as Commager observed: "It is scarcely an exaggeration to say that during the nineteenth century and well into the twentieth, religion prospered while theology slowly went bankrupt" (1950, 165). Morality superseded creed, a shift clearly seen in the most popular of all social gospel novels, *In His Steps*.

If these literary and cultural developments provided the general setting for the phenomenon of *In His Steps*, then William T. Stead's *If Christ Came to Chicago!* offered the immediate inspiration. Armed with statistics and interviews, the founder of Britain's *Review of Reviews* described the city's most glaring social injustices and challenged the citizens of Chicago to correct them through concerted political action. Part five of the book, entitled "What Would Christ Do in Chicago?", parallels the subtitle of Sheldon's novel, "What Would Jesus Do?". Sheldon's reliance upon Stead is clear from a concluding passage in Stead's book:

If Christ came to Chicago what would He wish me to do? That is the question with which I hope every reader will close this book. Nor is the answer difficult or far to seek. For what He would have you to do is to follow in His footsteps and be a Christ to those among whom you live, in the family, in the workshop, in the city and in the state (1894, 441).

Indeed, Stead recognized the similarity between his book and Sheldon's. The 1898 London edition of *If Christ Came to Chicago!* displayed the phrase "the precursor of *In His Steps*" beneath the title, and Stead said in the preface that Sheldon wrote *In His Steps* to popularize his ideas (Nicholl 1964, 30-31).

Sheldon never claimed that "What would Jesus do?" was an original question. Instead, he claimed that, as the essence of morality, the question was traditional. "It has been asked repeatedly by some of the best Christian men in the world," he wrote. "The Bishop of Exeter, many years ago, wrote a hymn which was sung in England by his people, and the last line of every stanza was 'What would Jesus do?' " (Crane 1909, 155).

Charles M. Sheldon (1857-1946) wrote *In His Steps* on the porch of his Topeka, Kansas house during the summer and fall of 1896. Sheldon was in the early years of his only full-time pastorate, which he held for some thirty-five years after graduating from Andover Theological Seminary and working as an intern in a small New England Church. His belief that Christian churches should solve the city's social problems had gained momentum in 1890 when, following an idea in Mrs. Humphrey Ward's *Robert Elsmere*, he had dressed in old clothes and tramped Topeka looking for a job (Gohdes 1954, 354). Looking everywhere but in tobacco shops and theaters, he finally found work shoveling snow from the ties and switches of the Santa Fe tracks. From his experience of looking for a job, Sheldon classified the population of Topeka into eight groups: doctors, lawyers, businessmen, railroad men, street car men, college students, journalists, and blacks. He then decided to spend ten more weeks observing blacks as closely as possible (Clark 1946, 29-30). Besides leading the 150 young people of his church to raise money to convert a black dance hall that served liquor into a sober library and reading room, Sheldon used his experiences and observations to illustrate his sermons, and these experiences served as background for *In His Steps* (Clark 1946, 8).

He wrote the novel to be read one chapter at a time during the Sunday evening service at Central Congregational Church, where he served as pastor from 1889 until 1924. Sheldon decided to write a series of sermons in narrative form for the evening services in an effort to stimulate church attendance. The high school and Washburn College students in his church, having already attended Sunday school and the morning worship service as well as an evening Christian Endeavor Society meeting, were abandoning vespers, so Sheldon thought that reading a serial story to them would revitalize attendance. His success was so great that he wrote twenty-five sermon serials in his first twenty-five years at Central Congregational. The first was *His Brother's Keeper*, a romance based on an iron miners' strike in the Upper Peninsula of Michigan. A cliff-hanger—the first chapter ends with the hero in the bottom of a mine which is flooding because the striking miners have removed the pumps—the story filled the church week after week and the students clamored for another. He subsequently wrote and delivered *Robert Hardy's Seven Days*, *The Crucifixion of Philip Strong*, *John King's Question Class*, *Edward Blake*, and *Born to Serve* (Sheldon 1938, 2-6). A.C. McClurg & Company published *The Crucifixion of Philip Strong* in 1895, and the Congregational Sunday School and Publishing Society in Boston published *His Brother's Keeper* two years later (Mott 1947, 194).

Sheldon's use of narrative from the pulpit was not his innovation. More than twenty years earlier, Harriet Beecher Stowe had complained about the plethora of serial novels, both religious and secular, that appeared after the Civil War:

Hath any one in our day, as in St. Paul's, a psalm, a doctrine, a tongue, a revelation, an interpretation—forthwith he wraps it up in a serial story, and presents it to the public. . . . Soon it will be necessary that every leading clergyman should embody in his theology a serial story, to be delivered from the pulpit Sunday after Sunday (1872, 2).

Apparently, Sheldon used a relatively conventional means to produce *In His Steps*.

The Story

In His Steps is a sort of turn-of-the-century New Testament. It begins with establishment religion being criticized by an unemployed laborer who dies after he reveals the true meaning of the scriptures to a congregation which had spurned him. But the Christ figure leaves a legacy. The novel tells of the lives of a dozen disciples, men and women who believe the man's interpretation and vow to live by real Christian principles. Although one of the twelve reneges, another replaces him and takes the message to another city. The message flourishes there as well, eventually spreading across the nation and even the world.

The Christ figure is Jack Manning, a typesetter in his early thirties who leaves New York after losing his job to a Linotype machine and ends up looking for employment in the railroad and meat-packing city of Raymond. His wife had died four months earlier of malnutrition and disease in a tenement, and his daughter is living with an employed friend while Manning hunts for a job. Starving, he cannot find work in Raymond, and the affluent members of First Church offer him neither direction nor hope. Manning's final public act is to confront the members of First Church with their hypocrisy during a Sunday morning service:

"I heard some people singing at a church prayer meeting the other night, 'All for Jesus, all for Jesus...,' and I kept wondering as I sat on the steps outside just what they meant by it. It seems to me there's an awful lot of trouble in the world that somehow wouldn't exist if all the people who sing such songs went and lived them out. I suppose I don't understand. But what would Jesus do? Is that what you mean by following His steps?" (p. 12)

After his speech, Manning collapses in the church of a heart attack. The minister takes him home and sends for his daughter, but the effort is tardy. Manning dies the following Sunday morning.

Henry Maxwell, minister of First Church, is the first to appropriate Manning's message. Manning's speech in First Church was, after all, a challenge based on Maxwell's sermon text, I Peter 2:21: "For to this you have been called, because Christ also suffered for you, leaving you an example, that you should follow in his steps." Although Maxwell had wished good luck to Manning, he had done nothing to help Manning find a job. Maxwell allows Manning to die in his house, but his conscience is disturbed.

The Sunday of Manning's death, Maxwell challenges his congregation to pledge to ask "What would Jesus do?" before doing anything. To his surprise, some fifty volunteers stay after the morning service to take the vow. For Maxwell, the first to take this pledge, the result is a continuous affront to his comfortable routine as pastor of an affluent church. Besides issuing the challenge to his congregation, which starts an abiding, if small and unsuccessful, movement in his congregation to force his resignation, Maxwell's pledge leads him to minister to laborers and the unemployed and to fight for Prohibition. In one case, Maxwell answers "What would Jesus do?" by using the money that he customarily spent on a European vacation to send a tenement family—an unemployed, suicidal father, his wife, who had lost three babies to disease, and four children, one who was sickly and another who was handicapped—for a week's vacation by the seashore in the home of a Christian woman.

Among the original fifty church members who take the pledge is Edward Norman, owner and editor of the Raymond *Daily News*. His pledge causes some drastic changes in both the appearance and the operation of the newspaper. Norman's first act as a Christian gatekeeper is to omit a three-and-a-half- column story about a highly publicized prize fight, presumably because of its brutality, but perhaps of the gambling integral to the sport. When the *Daily News* vendors are unable to sell the papers with such an omission, Norman buys the papers himself. Undaunted, he issues a number of Christian news policies, all in opposition to the contemporary yellow journalism of Pulitzer and Hearst. These include a ban on sensational and violent stories and on liquor and tobacco advertisements. Norman also refuses to print details of crime and gossip about famous persons, and he expands the Saturday edition so that he does not have to print one on Sunday. Norman institutes a profit-sharing plan, but without an audience of Christian readers and a substantial endowment, it is clear that his pledge will bankrupt his business.

Despite his doubtful prospects for success, Norman hires Fred Morris, whose vow had cost him his job as a reporter for the morning *Sentinel*. Morris had disobeyed his editor's order to skip church in order to get a scoop on a Sunday morning train robbery. Morris tells of his misfortune to Maxwell, who goes with him to Norman. Norman is delighted to hire a man with like sentiment.

The future of the *Daily News* is made secure by Virginia Page, whose vow has led her to ask, "What would Jesus do if he had inherited a million dollars?" The answer: Support Christian endeavors. She donates half of her fortune to the newspaper, and another $450 thousand to build a Christian settlement and rescue mission in the slums where she will work. Presumably, her ninety-five per cent charity will oil a camel's way through the eye of a needle.

Virginia Page's personal work in the slums leads her to help Loreen, a tent-meeting convert who reverts to drink shortly after taking the pledge. Finding Loreen drunk and confused, Page takes her home for recovery, prayer, and wholesome living. They attend tent meetings together. The slums turn violent on election night when local option is on the ballot, and someone hurls a liquor bottle at Virginia after the evening tent meeting. Loreen jumps in front of Virginia, taking the bottle's fatal blow. Loreen's vow leads her to the ultimate sacrifice, her life for her friend's.

Virginia's brother, Rollin Page, interprets his pledge otherwise. By the time that he vows to ask "What would Jesus do?" he has squandered almost half of his million-dollar inheritance on country club living. His charity consists of helping his sister build a rescue mission and keeping his club memberships current so that he can spread the gospel among the black tie set. As he tells his fiancée, who had refused his proposal before he took the pledge, "I know these men, their good and their bad qualities. I have been one of them.... I think I could possibly reach some of the young men and boys who have money and time to spend" (p. 112).

Rollin's fiancée is the talented soprano Rachel Winslow. Before taking the pledge, she had planned to accept a lucrative offer from a professional opera company, National Opera. Deciding that Jesus would not become a Caruso, she volunteers to sing in the tent meetings in the Rectangle, Raymond's tenement district. When her friend Virginia Page decides to build a Christian settlement there, Rachel Winslow volunteers to teach music to poor people at the settlement's Musical Institute, making her living from private music lessons.

Others pledge to do as they think Jesus would—Donald Marsh, President of Lincoln College and Professor of Philosophy and Ethics, enters politics to fight corruption and liquor; Milton Wright, a merchant who employs one hundred men, makes his business like a family by instituting profit-sharing; and Dr. West, a noted surgeon, donates his spare time to charity cases in the tenements—but none suffers as much for the pledge as does Alexander Powers. Powers, superintendent of the railroad shops in Raymond, discovers that his company is systematically violating state and federal anti-trust laws. Deciding that Jesus would blow the whistle, he hands over evidence to the authorities and resigns from his position, taking a lower-paying job as a telegraph operator, his former occupation. His honesty not only costs him his high income and corresponding social status, but it also estranges him from his wife and friends. *In His Steps* makes it clear that suffering is something that Jesus would do.

The person who will not suffer for the vow, the Judas of the twelve, is Jasper Chase, a successful novelist. He takes the pledge, but he refuses to sacrifice the fame and money that his socially useless novels bring to him. He rejects the vow deliberately:

Would He write this story? It was a social novel, written in a style that had proved popular. It has no purpose except to amuse. Its moral teaching was not bad, but neither was it Christian in any positive way.... When he had finished the last page of the last chapter of his book it was nearly dark. "What would Jesus do?" He had finally answered the question by denying his Lord (pp. 109-10).

Although many church members refuse to vow discipleship, only Chase reneges on the pledge.

If Jasper Chase is the disciple who betrays his commitment, then Calvin Bruce is his replacement who, like Paul, spreads the message to another city. Bruce, who attended seminary with Maxwell, visits Raymond for two weeks to observe the discipleship movement there. He becomes a believer, and challenges his congregation, Nazareth Avenue Church in Chicago, to take the What-would-Jesus-Do? vow. Although a hundred people do, Bruce believes that he can best fulfill his newfound commitment outside the established church. Edward, the Bishop, shares Bruce's belief, so they pool their savings to create a settlement in the slums, much as Virginia Page had done in Raymond. Across the street in a converted bar, Felicia Sterling, who took the pledge at Nazareth Avenue Church, establishes a housekeeping and cooking school for poor women, who need to learn "plain cooking, neatness, quickness, and a love of good work" (p. 164).

In His Steps closes with a vision that Maxwell has on his knees in prayer. He sees those who make their decisions after asking "What would Jesus do?" converting unbelievers and helping the less fortunate, often at the expense of harassment and ostracism. He sees Jasper Chase becoming more and more bitter even as he continues to write popular novels. He sees Rose Sterling, Felicia's sister who refused to take the vow, entering a loveless, baneful marriage for the sake of money and status. He also sees the gospel of discipleship spreading across the United States and throughout the world, the "dawn of the millennium of Christian history" (p. 188).

Because *In His Steps* proposes a method for Christian moral decision-making, examining the underlying belief system of this bestseller will reveal the version of Christianity that the novel champions. Questions that the narrative poses, such as "What would Jesus do if he were a millionaire?" and "What would Jesus do if he were Bishop of Chicago?", belie the novel's assumption that it merely restates New Testament Christianity—as if the Christianity of the New Testament itself was unified! Indeed, as Sheldon's contemporary Alfred Loisy argued in *The Gospel and the Church* (1903), Christianity has mutated throughout its history, shaping and being shaped by the various historical cultures in which Christian faith has made its home. To be sure, first-century Christianity bears familial resemblance to its twentieth-century namesake, but both necessarily bear the markings of their contemporary cultures. Twentieth-century American Christianity is not a displaced New Testament faith; it is marked by its culture as much as it marks its culture. Because *In His Steps* can reveal a cultural version of Christianity, a popular middle-class conception of religion, it deserves closer scrutiny.

Belief System

Because good is defined in terms of what Jesus would do in particular circumstances, it can be inferred that evil is whatever Jesus would not do, either in particular circumstances or under any circumstances. Discerning the nature of evil—or, for that matter, the nature of good—is difficult because *In His Steps* catalogs good and evil deeds without explaining why Jesus would do certain deeds and eschew others. The novel does not discuss the moral logic of Jesus; instead, it praises or condemns on the assumption that good and evil are recognizable *prima facie*. So in order to discover the nature of evil in this bestseller, to discover the rationale of condemnation, it is necessary to classify moral behaviors by comparing the acts that are praised as well as those that are denounced.

The first type of behavior that the novel condemns is the hypocrisy evident in the complacency and inaction of middle- and upper-class church members, people whose nonchalance toward the poor belies their support of the church. The evil of church hypocrisy is clear when Jack Manning asks church members to help him find work, and to a person they refuse. Manning exposes their hypocrisy when he interrupts the Sunday service to say,

I understand you can't all go out of your way to hunt up jobs for other people like me. I'm not asking you to; but what I feel puzzled about is, what is meant by following Jesus.... Do you mean that you are suffering and denying yourselves and trying to save the lost, suffering humanity just as I understand Jesus did? (p. 11)

Manning's soliloquy leads a number of people to pledge to imitate Jesus, which means in part to avoid hypocrisy by putting their piety into practice. Maxwell's first sermon after he pledges to preach as Jesus would contains a large measure of "rebuke for sin, especially hypocrisy" (p. 31). Rebuking hypocrisy is part of Maxwell's strategy of ending his own hypocrisy by overturning "the custom and habit of years in the ministry" (p. 50). Virginia Page reaches the same conclusion when she tells Rachel,

It maddens me to think that the society in which I have been brought up...is satisfied year after year to go on dressing and eating and having a good time, giving and receiving entertainments, spending money on houses and luxuries and occasionally, to ease its conscience, donating, without any personal sacrifice, a little money to charity (p. 38).

Hypocrisy's connection to complacency and inaction is clear in the narrative condemning Raymond's vote against local option:

More than a hundred professing Christian disciples had failed to go to the polls, and many more than that number had voted with the whiskey men. If all the church members of Raymond had voted against the saloon, it would today be outlawed instead of crowned king of the municipality" (p. 94).

Jesus was the Good Sufferer, so not to suffer is the supreme hypocrisy for the church member. Rachel understands this principle. As she explains to her mother why she must turn down a lucrative offer from a professional opera company in order to sing without remuneration in slum tent meetings, Rachel asks, "How much have we denied ourselves or given of our personal ease and pleasure to bless the place in which we live or imitate the life of the Saviour of the world?" (p. 47) Later she says, "I want to do something that will cost me something in the way of sacrifice. I am hungry to suffer something" (p. 71). The Chicago Bishop laments the unwillingness of the members of his diocese to suffer: "Martyrdom is a lost art with us. Our Christianity loves its ease and comfort too well to take up anything so rough and heavy as a cross" (p. 139). Indeed, the revulsion to suffering is illustrated in the suicide of Charles R. Sterling, a multi-millionaire from grain speculation and railroad ventures who contributed heavily to Nazareth Avenue Church. When Sterling learns of the collapse of his investments, of the loss of his fortunes "for which he himself had never really done an honest stroke of pure labor" (p. 142), he shoots himself. Suffering is the litmus test for Christian morality. Suffering, however, must be purposeful; it must be more than medieval self-flagellation. "Live in a simple, plain manner," Maxwell writes at the top of a list of what Jesus would do if he were Maxwell, "without undue asceticism" (p. 50). Those who will suffer for their beliefs are probably following Jesus; the unwillingness to suffer is an unchristian, or evil, attitude.

The hypocrisy of comfort, ease, and decorum is the evil of the rich. This point is important, because the novel's focus on hypocrisy as a central evil to overcome is directed at a wealthy, well-situated audience. Indeed, wealth and Christianity are interwoven in this tale; only two of the principle characters, Jack Manning and Loreen, are poor. Money, however, is both good and evil in this novel. It is a neutral tool that can support Christian activities, such as Virginia Page's endowment of the Christian newspaper and Maxwell's gift of a beach vacation for a poor family, or oppose Christian activities, as in the cases of gambling and Sunday income. This narrative identifies church members with wealth, and suggests church members are often, if not usually, poor stewards of their wealth.

The poor have their own evils. The rich are faulted for choosing to ignore the poor, whose morals reflect the squalor of the tenements. In his address to the First Church of Raymond, Jack Manning describes slums as places where children "grow up in misery, drunkenness, and sin" (p. 12). The Rectangle is "the coarse part of the sin of Raymond," a "stronghold of the devil" (p. 47) where "oaths and impurity and heavy drinking" (p. 63) accompany "crime" and "shame" (p. 70). Likewise, the slums of Chicago are an area of "spiritual destitution," "where vice and ignorance and shame and poverty were congested into hideous forms" (p. 149). The narrative never details the moral impurities of the poor, but it is clear that the slums are teeming with crime, drinking, and illicit sex. Apparently, poverty fosters immorality, while wealth hinders empathy. Thus the nature of evil in *In His Steps* is two-fold: satisfaction with the status quo among the wealthy and sensuality among the poor.

Just as there are two primary types of evil evident in *In His Steps*, there are two sources of evil in this novel. One involves the satisfaction with the status quo among well-to-do Christians. The root of complacency is greed, or selfishness, which ultimately contributes to the immorality of the tenements by corrupting the sources of social aid. The other source of evil is liquor, which is the most important link in the chain of poverty. Drinking leads to unemployment; unemployment leads to poverty; poverty leads to drinking. Selfishness and liquor are the attitude and the substance that cause complacency and sensuality.

Selfishness causes the satisfaction with the status quo among church members. The novel opens with Maxwell preparing a sermon on discipleship. He is interrupted by Jack Manning, who tells him that he is out of a job and asks for some direction. Manning suggests that the minister could refer him to someone in charge at the railroad—an interesting suggestion, given that the minister just happens to know the superintendent of the railroad shops and given that Manning is a typesetter by trade—but the minister is preoccupied with his sermon and irritated by the interruption, so he sends the tramp away. Before his conversion, Maxwell cares much more about his own work than about the plight of someone else. Maxwell's selfishness ends when he takes the vow. In his first sermon after his conversion, the minister denounces "the greed of wealth and the selfishness of fashion, two things that First Church had never heard rebuked this way before" (p. 31).

Selfishness is the attitude that must be resisted when facing the question, "What would Jesus do?". Edward Norman decides to christianize the Raymond *Daily News* even though he risks losing his livelihood by doing so. Alexander Powers blows the whistle on corporate corruption despite his inevitable loss of income and social position. Dr. West gives up his spare time by donating his services to indigents. Rachel Winslow sacrifices fame and fortune by singing for and working with the poor. Virginia Page gives away ninety-five per cent of her inheritance, while her brother Rollin loses some of his popularity by trying to convert the men of the clubs. (He tells Rachel, "A good many of them think I am a crank" [p. 113].) Milton Wright institutes profit-sharing for his employees even though he will probably take home less money from his business. Donald Marsh sacrifices the pleasure of scholastic seclusion in order to fulfill his civic responsibilities. Fred Morris refuses to work on Sunday, so he loses his job at the morning *Sentinel*. Only Jasper chase reneges on his vow, and he chooses fame over Christian purposefulness. The source of his choice, the cause of all unchristian acts, is selfishness.

The self-preoccupation of affluent church members permits the sensuality of the slums to fester. By their inattention to social problems, the wealthy churches are ultimately responsible for the sins of the poor. However, the immediate cause of slum immorality is liquor, which not only deadens moral inhibition but also keeps the poor unemployed and unemployable. Liquor keeps the poor poor.

Sensuality and unemployment are thus symptoms of alcoholism. For this reason, the social goal of Christian discipleship is Prohibition, first on a city-by-city basis, but ultimately on a national scale. When local option is put to a vote in Raymond, its importance as the great hope of the poor is well understood by Christian disciples. According to the narrative, "The Holy Spirit was battling with all His supernatural strength against the saloon devil which had so long held a jealous grasp on its slaves" (p. 77). Mr. Gray, long-time evangelist in the Rectangle, explains the futility of trying to convert the poor in the presence of taverns:

A good many of these poor creatures will go back again.... The environment does have a good deal to do with character. It does not stand to reason that these people can always resist the sight and smell of the devilish drink about them (p. 77).

Maxwell links taverns to crime and promiscuity when he asks his congregation, "Was there one word to be said by the Christian disciple, business man, citizen, in favor of continuing the license to crime and shame-producing institutions?" (p. 70).

Liquor and poverty are linked throughout *In His Steps*. Maxwell says that saloons cause crime and death (p. 54), and Marsh vows to fight the lawlessness and corruption of the saloon element (p. 73). Liquor "compassed" Loreen's degradation (p. 95). It is interesting that no rich character ever drinks—although the owners of the taverns are rich and sometimes even belong to churches. The case of Burns is the most explicit illustration of liquor causing poverty. The first time the Bishop met him, his drinking had kept him in the tenements, where his wife and child had perished in a fire. The Bishop found him a job, but Burns lost it because he continued to drink. Even when the Bishop hires Burns, the temptation to drink nearly ruins him again. The Bishop broods about the neighboring saloon: "It stood there, and all the others lined the street like so many traps set for Burns. How long would the man be able to resist the smell of the damnable stuff?" (p. 162).

In His Steps suggests that the poor cannot master their own destiny. They are at the mercy of their environment, unlike the rich, who must learn to master their personal desires. The rich can change themselves; the poor cannot. Unless the rich outlaw liquor, the poor will be doomed to living in squalor and immorality.

In His Steps proposes a top-down solution to the problem of the immorality of the slums: rescue by the affluent. Most of the evils in the novel are acts or attitudes that can be conquered only by the rich: hypocrisy (the rich need a change of heart and the resolve to carry through), drinking (the rich must vote to outlaw liquor), Sunday work (business owners should change their policies), gambling (the novel focuses on stocks and futures, activities in which only persons of means can engage), and disloyalty (political leaders are often corrupt and negligent of the poor). The affluent, of course, must conquer their selfishness. Maxwell says, "No one ever lived who had succeeded in overcoming selfishness like Jesus. If men followed Him regardless of results the world would at once begin to enjoy a new life" (p. 174). From the beginning to the end of the novel, the poor must wait for the conversion of the rich. They cannot lift themselves from their economic and moral abyss; no leader emerges from the rank and file to help end the plight of the poor. Instead, they must seek aid from the powers that be or, more often, wait for the powers that be to act on their own accord.

Very occasionally the poor do take the initiative to seek help. Jack Manning goes to Reverend Maxwell's house to ask the minister for a job referral. The minister is cordial but uncooperative, so one needy person who acts on his own initiative is thwarted. Another unemployed man confesses to having begged:

I have begged, and I have been to charity institutions, and I have done everything when out of a job except steal and lie in order to get food and fuel. I don't know as Jesus would have done some of the things I have been obliged to do for a living, but I know I have never knowingly done wrong when out of work. Sometimes I think maybe He would have starved sooner than beg. I don't know (p. 177).

But begging is atypical. The poor usually wait for the affluent to come to them. This is the case with Loreen, who had not recognized the immorality of her habitual drunkenness and sexual promiscuity until she "had tasted of the joy of a better life" (p. 80) during an evangelical tent meeting in the slums conducted by a professional evangelist and a number of First Church do-gooders. The very next day Loreen backslides, but Virginia Page discovers her and takes Loreen home with her. Loreen can resist temptation only "with a young lady from the society circles up town supporting her" (p. 81).

The weakness of the poor is seen again later in the novel. As two men hold up the Bishop of Chicago, one of them, Burns, recognizes the Bishop. The Bishop had prayed for his soul and had found a job for him as a warehouse foreman on the condition that he quit drinking. He continued to drink, however, and he turned to crime after losing the job that the Bishop had found for him. Once again the Bishop prays and offers to find employment for them if they will stop drinking. They agree, and the Bishop finds Burns' companion a job as a driver for a manufacturer of drays, and he hires Burns as a janitor at the settlement. The very next day Burns falters, nearly entering a nearby bar, but the Bishop stops him. Like Loreen, Burns is unable to resist temptation without help from a guardian from the upper classes.

The ineptitude of the poor comes into focus with their ingratitude, which turns into verbal scorn and violence. Although the affluent are trying to improve the situation of the poor—in large measure by outlawing liquor—the poor do not appreciate these efforts. The evening of the vote on local option "the Rectangle was drunk and enraged.... 'Down with the aristocrats!' shouted a shrill voice, more like a woman's than a man's. A shower of mud and stones followed" (p. 93). Someone hurls a heavy bottle at Virginia Page, but it strikes and kills Loreen, who had rejected the slum's way of life. The poor resent their only source of social salvation.

Late in the narrative the poor are described in detail. At the invitation of the Bishop and Dr. Bruce, Maxwell visits the settlement hall in Chicago to explain Christian discipleship to the poor there. He addresses "men out of work, wretched creatures who had lost faith in God and man, anarchists and infidels, free-thinkers and no-thinkers," representing "all the city's worst, most hopeless, most dangerous, depraved elements" (p. 172). These are people typified by "scorn of creeds, hatred of the social order, desperate narrowness and selfishness" (p. 174). After Maxwell's speech, a number of the men in the audience stand up to denounce the causes of social injustice; they cite capitalism, unfair taxes, churches, courts, big business, and technology. The wrongheadedness of these notions becomes apparent when Rachel Winslow sings a hymn. Even the most hostile men cry or become pensive. Instead of blaming their plight on social forces, they need to believe and act according to the gospel:

The Bishop said that night while Rachel was singing that if the world of sinful, diseased, depraved, lost humanity could only have the gospel preached to it by consecrated prima donnas and professional tenors and altos and bassos, he believed it would hasten the coming of the Kingdom quicker than any other one force (p. 179).

The lost poor must learn to accept both the material and ideology that the affluent provide.

Besides retraining the poor in rescue missions, the enlightened need to cleanse the cities through political power. The system that exists is just and need not be changed; it is the leadership, the individuals in control, who must be replaced. Political change, that is, is neither systemic nor structural, but individual. Donald Marsh recognizes his responsibility as an individual, as he tells Maxwell:

I understand that our city officials are a corrupt, unprincipled set of men, controlled in large part by the whiskey element and thoroughly selfish so far as the affairs of city government are concerned.... My plain duty is to take

a personal part in this coming election, go to the primaries, throw the weight
of my influence, whatever it is, toward the nomination and election of good
men (p. 72).

Marsh never says who he favors, but there is no mention of
nominating someone with first-hand experience of poverty. Most
assuredly, good leadership comes from among the well-to-do.

In contrast to the policies of Progressivism, deliverance from
the immoralities that accompany poverty is not to be found in
government programs or private agencies. These are helpful only
insofar as they are directed by Christian leaders acting as Jesus
would; otherwise, they are susceptible to corruption. Christianity
here is not to be confused with churches, because the churches are
rife with hypocrisy. Rather, true Christianity is to be found among
the disciples within the churches. Deliverance from the evils of
hypocrisy and sensuality occurs when enlightened individuals work
for the good of everyone within the democratic system. But
democracy here does not imply equality, reciprocity, or
interdependence; the system is hierarchical. Individuals are elevated
to positions of power by the system which allows the degradation
of classes of people. Deliverance is imperative but voluntary, and
always paternal and patronizing. The destiny of the poor rests in
the hands of the Christian rich.

If the scandal in the novel is that a self-satisfied church has
permitted the society to be corrupted and split by a plague of
selfishness and sensuality, then the resolution in the novel is a vision
of individual purposefulness and community life. In this regard,
the novel is rule-utilitarian. The greatest good for the greatest
number, the end that is sought, is social harmony, and the means
of achieving this goal is to instill individuals with a sense of purpose.
Purpose, of course, is singularly Christian, and it finds embodiment
in a number of proscriptions: do not drink, do not gamble, and
do not cheat, for example. Put positively, such principles as sobriety
and honest work, derivatives of Christian purposefulness, will
produce social unity.

The ideal of community is evident in Maxwell's waking vision
that he has during prayer at the end of the novel. He sees the church
in the United States bonded by a common theme:

He thought he saw the church of Jesus in America open its heart to the moving of the Spirit and rise to the sacrifice of its ease and self-satisfaction in the name of Jesus. He thought he saw the motto, "What would Jesus do?" inscribed over every church, and written on every church member's heart (p. 188).

Maxwell's vision of a united church extends overseas as well when he sees "the Endeavor Societies all over the world carrying in their great processions at some mighty convention a banner on which was written, 'What would Jesus do?' " (p. 188). The call of discipleship had already created growing communities of disciples in Raymond and Chicago. The ideal of community remained to be fulfilled across the nation and even the world.

Although the novel does not propose social equality as a goal, it does argue that the rich should feel empathy for the poor. Manning pleads for such empathy when he interrupts the Sunday morning service at the beginning of the novel, and Maxwell carries Manning's torch throughout the narrative. In his final sermon, Maxwell tells the congregation that doing what Jesus would involves having genuine concern for the welfare of the disadvantaged. He asks, "Would He take rentals from saloons and other disreputable property, or even from tenement property that was so constructed that the inmates had no such things as a home and no such possibility as privacy or cleanliness?" (p. 182).

Maxwell was referring to Clarence Penrose, who owned tenements in an area of Chicago called the Penrose District. After taking the vow, Penrose had begun to feel uneasy about being a slumlord. His uneasiness climaxed one morning when he read in the newspaper that one of his tenants had been killed while stealing a lump of coal. The thief had been unemployed for six months, and his wife and six children were huddled in a three-room apartment. The newspaper article horrified him and left him sleepless. Pale and sobbing, Penrose sought the Bishop's advice with "almost a child's terror in his voice" (p. 169). The Bishop accompanied him to the home of the dead man's family, and from that day, Penrose took better care of his tenants. Through empathy, Penrose established a bond with the poor. The poor may not achieve economic parity with the rich—community does not imply equality—but as Penrose illustrates, there can be a bond between rich and poor.

This bond apparently has only limited applications to personal relationships. There is interaction between the rich and poor in *In His Steps*, but only in one case does this interaction approach friendship, and even here the text is ambivalent. Virginia Page finds Loreen (the poor seldom have last names) drunk the day after Loreen had made a confession of faith at a revival meeting, and remembering that Jesus was a friend of publicans and sinners, decides to remove the street urchin from the environment of temptation. Virginia takes Loreen home with her. Virginia's grandmother is appalled, and when Virginia refuses to put the poor girl out, Madam Page packs her bags and heads south to stay with her brothers and sisters. When Virginia asks her brother if she did the right thing, he replies,

If you think this poor creature owes her safety and salvation to your personal care, it was the only thing for you to do. Oh Virginia, to think that we have all these years enjoyed our beautiful home and all these luxuries selfishly, forgetful of the multitudes like this woman! Surely, Jesus in our places would do what you have done (p. 84).

Virginia befriends Loreen because she needs help and for no other reason. The relationship is only apparently a friendship. It is an I-It act of rehabilitation rather than an I-Thou relationship of mutuality.

A closer bond should be established between employers and their employees, according to the text. At the end of his list entitled, "What Jesus would probably do in Milton Wright's place as a business man," the employer described the community to be established within the workplace, between businesses, and in the society at large:

The principle of unselfishness and helpfulness in the business would direct all its details. Upon this principle he would shape the entire plan of his relations to his employees, to the people who were his customers and to the general business world with which he was connected (p. 62).

The direct result of this principle was the institution of profit-sharing, which Wright believed would lead the employees "to feel a personal share in the profits of the business and, more than that, a personal love for themselves on the part of the firm" (p. 62). Community in the workplace is recognized by Norman of the *News*, too. He believed that Jesus would operate a newspaper "on some loving family plan, where editors, reporters, pressmen and all meet to discuss and devise and plan" (p. 29). To Jesus, business is a place of mutual support.

Christian discipleship can also establish community on a scale far removed from the city or the workplace. The ideal is present in romantic relationships as well. The beautiful Rachel Winslow is pursued by Jasper Chase and Rollin Page. Until her vow, she favors Jasper, whose first novel was a thinly veiled account of their romance. However, after Rachel becomes a disciple, she finds Jasper less attractive. After an emotional service in the Rectangle, Jasper proposes to Rachel, thereby revealing the insincerity of his vow. Repulsed, Rachel declines. As she explains to Virginia:

> He touched my emotions, and I admired his skill as a writer. I have thought at times that I cared a good deal for him. I think perhaps if he had spoken to me at any other time than the one he chose, I could easily have persuaded myself that I loved him. But not now (p. 102).

Virginia's other suitor, Rollin, also proposes, but she turns him down as well because he has not vowed to follow the steps of Jesus. She tells him, "I do not and I cannot love you because you have no purpose in life.... You spend your time in club life, in amusements, in travel, in luxury. What is there in such life to attract a woman?" (p. 44). But Rollin does convert, and his persistence pays off. After discussing his evangelism of the rich with him, she thinks, "I am beginning to know what it means to be loved by a noble man. I shall love Rollin Page after all" (p. 113). In Maxwell's prophetic vision, he sees the couple married and mutually determined to follow "His steps with an eagerness intensified and purified by their love for each other" (p. 187).

The answer to selfishness and sensuality is purpose and social harmony, goals achieved through the activities of Christian disciples. Purpose is individual, and harmony of the classes implies satisfaction with one's social position. Clearly, *In His Steps* advocates instilling a sense of middle-class manners in the poor without endowing them with middle-class material resources.

Because *In His Steps* assumes a causal connection between belief and behavior, belief needs to be christianized before the social order can be christianized. In other words, the primary step to resolving the evils that result from selfishness and sensuality is conversion to Christian discipleship. Discipleship is identified with asking "What would Jesus do?", a question which yields applications almost mechanically. The applications are individual involvement in social and political work as well as evangelism. Put simply, this bestseller proposes that evil can be overcome by converted individuals applying a formula to social problems.

The primacy of belief is revealed in Maxwell's first speech to pledge volunteers after the previous week's episode with Jack Manning. He says, "The experience I have been through since last Sunday has left me so dissatisfied with my previous definition of Christian discipleship that I have been compelled to take this action" (p. 17). The minister reconceptualizes his beliefs and persuades others to do so as well before he proposes any concrete action, such as fighting for prohibition.

Maxwell also makes it clear that the vow is voluntary and subject to individual interpretation. In the same speech he says, "I will of course include myself in this company of volunteers...and will not oppose whatever is done if they think Christ would do it" (p. 16). Upon hearing Rachel sing in a tent meeting at the Rectangle, Maxwell "had a glimpse of something that Jesus would probably do with a voice like Rachel Winslow's" (p. 53). Rachel tells her mother, "I judge no one else; I condemn no other professional singer. I simply decide my own course. As I look at it, I have a conviction that Jesus would do something else" (p. 46). After Powers blows the whistle on corporate corruption, Maxwell tells his wife that he thinks Jesus would have done the same thing, adding, "At any rate, Powers has decided so and each one of us who made the promise understands that he is not deciding Jesus' conduct for anyone else, only for himself" (p. 58). In a letter to a friend of his describing the discipleship movement in Raymond, Dr. Bruce says,

So far no one has interpreted the spirit of Jesus in such a way as to abandon his earthly possessions, give away of his wealth, or in any literal way imitate the Christians of the order, for example, of St. Francis of Assisi. It was the unanimous consent, however, that if any disciple should feel that Jesus in his own particular case would do that, there could be only one answer to the question (pp. 121-22).

Thus is discipleship subject to individual interpretation.

However, discipleship has a formula. To answer the question "What would Jesus do?" individuals follow three steps: prayer, Bible study, and fellowship. Prayer is designed to give the individual the feeling that he or she is making the correct decision. Prayer leads neither to miracles nor to knowledge, but rather to emotional comfort. At the beginning of the first discipleship meeting at First Church, Maxwell prays:

And almost with the first syllable he uttered there was a distinct presence of the Spirit felt by them all. As the prayer went on, this presence grew in power. They all felt it. The room was filled with it as plainly as if it had been visible.... If an audible voice from heaven had sanctioned their pledge to follow the Master's steps, not one person present could have felt more certain of the divine blessing (p. 17).

During that meeting, Rachel asks Maxwell how to determine what Jesus would do, given that the Bible does not address every situation that someone can face, and Maxwell replies that confirmation comes through prayer. His answer is given credibility by the feeling that results from the meeting's prayer of benediction: "And again as before the Spirit made Himself manifest. Every head remained bowed a long time. They went away finally in silence. There was a feeling that prevented speech" (p. 19). In other words, prayer makes a person feel good about his or her decision.

The importance of emotional comfort is underscored throughout the narrative. When Maxwell prays with Mr. Gray, a professional evangelist who works in the Rectangle, "Gray was touched to tears" (p. 51). As Felicia prays with her bedridden mother, "the invalid was weeping softly and her nervous tension was over" (p. 133). After Dr. Bruce takes the vow and prays from his Nazareth Avenue Church pulpit, "a distinct wave of spiritual power moved over the congregation. The most careless persons in the church felt it. Felicia, whose sensitive religious nature responded swiftly to every touch of emotion, quivered" (pp. 133-34). Prayers punctuate the activities of the disciples, suggesting that ethical decisions are validated as much by emotion as by reason.

If prayer is the first step in deciding what Jesus would do, then Bible study is probably the second. The importance of Bible study in this narrative, however, is more implied than stated. When Rachel says, "I am a little in doubt as to the source of knowledge concerning what Jesus would do.... There are many perplexing questions in our civilization that are not mentioned in the teachings of Jesus" (pp. 17-18), she is affirming the importance of the New Testament while also pointing out its limitations. Never does a character pore through the New Testament in search of biblical parallels to contemporary problems, but the numerous quotations and paraphrases in the text suggest that the theme of the novel, as well as the specific decisions made in it by the characters, do pass biblical muster. Ten of the novel's thirty-one chapters begin with a verse from the New Testament, and the characters quote Bible passages at will. A complement to Rachel's statement is found later in one by Virginia:

"I think we are beginning to understand," said Virginia, "the meaning of that command, 'Grow in the grace and knowledge of our Lord and Savior Jesus Christ.' I am sure I do not know all that He would do in detail until I know Him better" (p. 107).

The quotation from II Peter in this context shows that the Bible is necessary but insufficient, that moral guidance requires emotional reassurance as well as knowledge of the Bible.

Answering the question "What would Jesus do?" has one more ingredient: comradeship. Although the moral choices of disciples are individual, they are by no means private. Those who take the vow habitually seek the opinions of other enlightened Christians even though they claim that they are free to ignore the suggestions of others. When Marsh asks Maxwell whether discipleship will produce uniform agreement, Maxwell responds, "No; I don't know that we can expect that. But when it comes to a genuine, honest, enlightened following of Jesus' steps, I cannot believe there will be any confusion either in our own minds or in the judgment of others" (p. 18). The narrative suggests that the vow will produce plurality, but there is universal conformity of opinion among the enlightened which Dr. Bruce refers to as "a fellowship, not of creed but of conduct" (p. 123). The text abounds with examples of consensus seeking, "seeking light from one another" (p. 33). Virginia discusses wealth with Rachel:

Virginia was rapidly reaching a conclusion with respect to a large part of her money. She had talked it over with Rachel and they had been able to agree that if Jesus had a vast amount of money at His disposal He might do with some of it as Virginia planned. At any rate they felt that whatever He might do in such case would have as large an element of variety in it as the differences in persons and circumstances. There could be no one fixed Christian way of using money. The rule that regulated its use was unselfish utility (p. 76).

Maxwell observes that the disciples at First Church "seemed drawn very close together by a bond of common fellowship that demanded and enjoyed mutual confidences. It was the general feeling that the spirit of Jesus was the spirit of very open, frank confession of experience" (p. 85).

The three-step process of moral decision-making—finding biblical, emotional, and community support—yields two types of Christian action: evangelism and social work. The gospel of Christian discipleship must be preached to the ends of the earth. Maxwell makes a modest beginning at First Church; believers spread the message to the country clubs and to the Rectangle; endeavor societies make disciples in Raymond and then across the country; Nazareth Avenue Church hears the message in Chicago; and Dr. Bruce and the Bishop take the gospel to the poor in their settlement house in the Chicago slums. Norman's newspaper becomes "one of the real factors of the nation to mold its principles and actually shape its policy" (p. 187). In his vision at the end of the novel, Maxwell "thought he saw the motto, 'What would Jesus do?' inscribed over every church door, and written on every church member's heart" (p. 188).

Social work is the necessary complement to evangelism. It has various manifestations, many of which are designed to raise the standards of the poor or to keep the poor from harming themselves. Felicia brings home cooking to the ghettos, Rachel teaches the poor to sing, Virginia runs a rescue mission, and all the disciples vote against liquor. The effectiveness of this social work is revealed in Maxwell's vision:

He saw Burns and his companion and a great company of men like them, redeemed and giving in turn to others, conquering their passions by the divine grace, and proving by their daily lives the reality of the new birth even in the lowest and most abandoned (p. 188).

His three steps—Bible study, prayer, and counsel—lead to evangelism and social work and finally to measurable social effects. In this way individualistic philanthropy produces emotional satisfaction and community.

After In His Steps

After Sheldon read *In His Steps* chapter by chapter to his evening congregation, the Chicago *Advance*, a Congregational weekly, paid $75 for serial rights to the story. Apparently Sheldon's other serial novels had not sold well, because two publishers, McClurg and Fleming H. Revell, turned the novel down. According to Tebbel, "Sheldon...virtually begged Revell to publish his work, but the publisher rejected it not once but three times on the ground that it was too revolutionary, too 'practical' " (1975, 333). Sheldon convinced the *Advance* to publish the serial as a book. Unfamiliar with book publishing, the *Advance* filed an incomplete application for copyright, making the copyright defective and leaving the book in the public domain. Sheldon said that the *Advance* issued more than one hundred thousand copies by June 1897 (1925, 98). By 1899, *Advance* had four editions of the book for sale, priced at ten, twenty-five, forty, and seventy-five cents, and an illustrated version for $1.25.

The novel's defective copyright together with its demonstrated popularity attracted more than a dozen publishing pirates, who issued the book in a variety of editions without paying any royalties whatsoever.[1] Even Revell, which had steadfastly resisted Sheldon's offer to publish the story, joined the troop of publishers who issued the title. Sheldon told of one New York firm which bought paperback editions from *Advance* and resold them for twenty-five cents with cloth covers. The company also purchased unbound sheets from *Advance* to bind and sell for fifty cents until it finally set the novel in type itself. Ten editions appeared in 1899, varying in price from twenty-five cents to a dollar (Sheldon 1938, 8). Before Sheldon's death in 1946, at least eighteen American publishers issued the title, which was sold in bookstores, by mail, and even door-to-door (Sheldon 1925, 99; Knight 1951, 123):

Advance Publishing Co. (1897), H.M. Caldwell (1899), Smith-Andrews (1899, apparently authorized by Advance), D.C. Cook (1899), Street & Smith (1899), Altemus (1899), Western News Company (1899), Ketcham (1899), Munro (1899), Ogilvie (1899), Revell (1899), Laird & Lee (1900), Burt (1910?), Christian Herald (1920, certainly authorized), Sears (1923), Grosset & Dunlap, Winston Books, Inc. (1943) (Mott 1947, 195).

The novel's popularity in the United States was matched if not bettered in England. Some thirty British publishers issued editions of *In His Steps*, ranging from penny paperbacks to holiday editions priced at eight and a half shillings. Some of the editions were even revised to correct the theological mistakes in the original, as was the case in Mrs. J.B. Horton's revision entitled *The Rescue of Loreen.* Religious magazines such as the *British Weekly* debated the novel's theological soundness, as did numbers of ministers from their pulpits. Some ministers even distributed the novel to their entire congregations (Sheldon 1925, 100-101).

Sheldon reported that his novel prompted thousands of readers to write to him, mostly praising or chiding him for his message (1942, 120-26). Hundreds, he said, responded to the phenomenal sales of the book, thinking that Sheldon himself was reaping a bounty in royalties. Readers with a variety of maladies and hardships asked Sheldon to behave as Jesus would by sharing his wealth with them. These letters, he said,

began or closed the appeal for financial help by saying, "Brother, take it to your heart, what would Jesus do? Surely you cannot imagine Him clinging to the wealth you have received from your book. He would surely share it with others who are in need. You cannot imagine him refusing my request. What would Jesus do?" (1925, 103)

These appeals for financial assistance illustrate both the great sales of the book as well as the resonance of its message. (The theme of following the steps of Jesus also inspired muckrakers like Lincoln Steffens. In his articles and books, Steffens illustrated universal corruption, the human condition overcome solely by faith and the emulation of Jesus [Steel 1980, 38]).

Sheldon complained that the pirated editions "took from the author every right he had in the work of his own brain and heart" (1925, 104). Sheldon did receive royalties, however, even if they were relatively meager. The Advance Publishing Company paid him a ten per cent royalty, or about one thousand dollars from the hundred thousand ten-cent copies that Sheldon said the firm sold. Sheldon later sold whatever book rights he held to Advance for another one hundred dollars. Even some pirates mailed checks to him. Grosset and Dunlap of New York sent him another thousand dollars, and the Bowden Publishing company of London sent him one hundred dollars. Sheldon said that the other publishers paid him nothing (1925, 104; 1938, 8-9).

Two years after *In His Steps* was first published in the United States, the novel was translated into foreign languages. Sheldon said that he had copies of the novel in Armenian, Bulgarian, Danish,

Dutch, Esperanto, Gaelic, a Hindu dialect, Hungarian, French, German, Greek, Italian, Japanese, Norwegian, Persian, Russian, Spanish, Swedish, Turkish, and Welsh. Sheldon said that the Persian translator used an English edition as a textbook for college English classes in a Presbyterian mission, and that the Russian edition was used in classrooms in the United States. He also said that churches in Sweden, Mexico, and Wales studied the book for religious rather than academic purposes. The translation and study of the book abroad suggests that this bestseller served an evangelical function, spreading the belief system of middle-class individualism abroad (1925, 105-107).

Besides being published around the world, *In His Steps* was also converted into a stage play and into a motion picture. F. H. Lane, a drama instructor at Washburn College, wrote the play with Sheldon, which was then endorsed by the Drama League of America and first performed in Sheldon's Central Congregational Church in Topeka. Lane sold the script privately to churches and schools across the country (1938, 19-20). In 1936, the Grand National Film Corporation released a film loosely based on the novel, which showed to audiences in England and the United States (Sheldon 1938, 21-22).

Sheldon said that the popularity of *In His Steps* surprised him. Shortly after the novel was published, Sheldon received a telegram from *Advance* saying that it had sold ten thousand copies. Sheldon said that he remarked to his wife, "Wouldn't it be wonderful if the story went up to 15,000 copies?" (1925, 100). His surprise turned to bitterness, however, as he learned that the novel succeeded mostly at the hands of pirates. Regarding the sales of the novel through Woolworth's, Sheldon commented, "I have never received anything, because, after all, business is business" (Sheldon 1938, 11). After learning that the Spanish translator changed the protagonist's name from Henry Maxwell to Henry Ford, Sheldon said, "I have sometimes felt that Henry ought to give me a new car because the book is selling all over South America, giving him free advertising such as he never had before" (Sheldon 1938, 17). Regarding the movie version, he groused, "Of course I have received nothing from all this showing, and would not take a cent from its box office receipts if it mounted into the millions" (Sheldon 1938, 21). Sheldon created a popular culture gold mine, and he was furious that its fortunes were beyond his control.

In 1925 Sheldon wrote that he was astonished to learn that his novel was still in print. J.H. Sears, who owned a small publishing company in Kingsport, Tennessee, told Sheldon that he had sold more than 150 thousand copies of a ten-cent paperback edition through Woolworth's (109-10; 1938, 10-11). In 1947, Mott estimated sales of the novel at six million copies and offered this comment: "As literature, it is nothing less than amateurish; as a social document, it has first-rate importance" (p. 197). Given that *In His Steps* still sells at a rate of nearly thirty thousand copies per year ("Best-Selling Backlist Books" 1984, 103), Mott's assessment is beyond question.

In 1900, Sheldon was given the opportunity to follow Jesus in the newspaper business. The Topeka *Capital* challenged Sheldon to edit the newspaper for a week according to the illustration of Edward Norman in the novel. Sheldon did, and under his authority, the newspaper printed all articles and editorials with bylines, omitted coverage of scandals, crimes, and brutal sports, and refused advertising for liquor, patent medicine, tobacco, and women's underwear (Cordova 1967, 93-95). Circulation went from a normal twelve thousand to an extraordinary 360 thousand, keeping presses in Chicago and New York as well as Topeka working overtime to satisfy the curiosity of buyers across the country. Mott described the "Sheldon Edition" as "virtuous," but "undeniably dull." J.K. Hudson, the editor, promised his readers that the paper would return to its former policies (Mott 1947, 197).

Hart suggests that the meaning of Sheldon's popularity lay in the novel's proposal of a simple solution to the complex moral and social issues of the day (1954, 312). Boyer, however, argues that *In His Steps* has more to do with the middle class psyche at the turn of the century than with religion or social reform. He says that the middle class was experiencing profound anxiety over the possibility of violence erupting from the lower classes:

The shorthand symbol for this violent potential is alcohol. The central Prohibition argument in *In His Steps* is not the wasted money, the political corruption, the health hazard, the broken homes, or any of the other usual appeals; it is rather the belief that liquor *inflames* the workers, increasing the likelihood that they will burst out of control and unleash the ugly violence which is assumed to see the just below the surface of working-class communities (1971, 68).

This element is present in the novel, but not to the degree that Boyer suggests. Indeed, if the fear of violence is to be read into the significance of the novel at all, it is simply to highlight the need to convert faith into socially relevant morality. More than fear in the middle-class psyche, the novel illustrates guilt about middle-class religion as well as trust in enlightened individualism. In this sense, *"In His Steps* offers a remarkably revealing glimpse into the American middle-class mind at the turn of the last century, as filtered through the consciousness of Charles M. Sheldon" (Boyer 1971, 78).

Shortly before his death, the elderly Charles Sheldon told a religious writer what he thought Jesus would do. He named three things. First, he said, Jesus would have the churches "promote World Brotherhood. That would mean a Christian Union against war, and against social differences." Second, Jesus would battle alcohol, which, "next to war, is our worst enemy." Finally, Jesus would preserve the nuclear family, "the oldest and most important institution of the human race" (Clark 1946, 11). Fifty years after he delivered *In His Steps* to his congregation in Topeka, Sheldon still believed that it was up to the churches to instill the values of community and sobriety into the unredeemed world at large, one individual at a time.

Chapter Three

"Ralph Connor's" Frontier Religion

A year after *In His Steps* was published, another minister's novel, *Black Rock,* became a bestseller in the United States. In many respects, these novels are very different. *In His Steps* employs an urban setting, focuses on the beneficence of the affluent, and advocates an individualistic formula for moral decision-making; *Black Rock* takes place in the mountains of western Canada, emphasizes the deep-down goodness of the working class, and stresses the social nature of God's providence. Both, however, see selfishness as the chief impediment to Prohibition, a policy which, according to these texts, would go far towards creating wholesome communities. *Black Rock* is single-minded on this theme, suggesting that the cure to social problems rests in individual faith and its companion, social morality.

The author of *Black Rock* is "Ralph Connor," the pen name of the Reverend Charles William Gordon, who wrote nearly thirty religious novels mostly set in the Canadian west. His mother was Mary Robertson Gordon, former philosophy teacher at Mt. Holyoke and cousin of Andrew Murray, the renowned mystic of the Dutch Reformed South African Church. His father was the Reverend Daniel Gordon, Presbyterian missionary among Canada's Scottish immigrants (*The Critic* 1900, 311). Gordon was born in 1860 in Glengarry, now called Alexandria, fifty miles from Montreal, the site of Connor's popular Glengarry tales. When he was ten years old, his family moved to Harrington, in Western Ontario, where his love for English, mathematics, and the classics eventually won him high honors at St. Mary's Collegiate Institute, from which he graduated in 1878. After graduation, Gordon taught in a country school for a year and a half before enrolling at the University of

Toronto. In 1883, he graduated with honors in classics from Toronto, where his developing social consciousness led him to advocate that the university admit women. Afterwards he taught high school for a year, then began his theological studies at Knox College of the University of Toronto, from which he graduated in 1887 after fulfilling the Presbyterian Church's ministers' missionary requirement in Manitoba, organizing Sunday schools, Bible studies, and church sports teams in southern Manitoba. Gordon spent the following year studying at Edinburgh University, then returned to Canada to pursue his career as a missionary (Adams 1913, 109-10).

Gordon began his writing career in 1897 when he produced a pamphlet on Western Canada entitled *Beyond the Marshes* for the Westminster Company, a Presbyterian publishing firm. Four years earlier, he had been transferred from Banff, Alberta, where he had been stationed for two years as a missionary among railroaders, miners, and ranchers, to St. Stephen's Church in Winnipeg, Manitoba to work as a pastor among the immigrants there. *Beyond the Marshes* was based upon his observations during that period.

Black Rock

The social nature of Gordon's work in Winnipeg also provided the basis for his first novel, *Black Rock: A Tale of the Selkirks* (1898), which became a bestseller in the United States. The impetus for writing the novel was Gordon's trip to Toronto to appeal to the Presbyterian Church Committee on Western Missions to help western Canadian farmers whose wheat crops had been devastated for four consecutive years. The Reverend James A. Macdonald, editor of *Westminster Magazine,* suggested that Gordon support the western cause by writing a short story about frontier life for the Christmas issue. Ten days later Gordon submitted a description of western lumber camps to Macdonald. "My sole purpose was to awaken my church in Eastern Canada to the splendor of the mighty religious adventure being attempted by the missionary pioneers in the Canada beyond the Great Lakes," Gordon later recalled (1938, 148).

Although Macdonald liked "Christmas in a Lumber Camp," he thought that it was too long, so he asked Gordon to revise the sketch into a sequence of three installments. This Gordon did, and the three short stories, "Tales from the Selkirks," became the first third of *Black Rock*, the novel. Macdonald then asked for two more sets of related short stories. After Gordon complied, crafting a novel out of this series of short stories, Macdonald made the rounds of New York publishers, who summarily rejected the novel because they said that its advocacy of religion and temperance would restrict its sales and because they appeared to be more interested in publishing books about the current Spanish-American War. Undaunted, Macdonald published the novel himself through the Westminster presses.

It was Macdonald who was the source of Gordon's pseudonym. Because fiction writing was an activity that a minister, particularly the secretary of the home mission board, could not do respectably, Macdonald asked Gordon to supply a pen name with the original submission. Gordon telegraphed "Cannor," which he derived from British *Can*adian *Nor*thwest Mission, the mission board's name appearing on his letterhead. The telegraph operator "corrected" the spelling to "Connor," and the bewildered editor added the first name. Thus it was that this Scotch Presbyterian assumed an Irish name (Gordon 1938, 148-49).

Publishing pirates, stymied by the international copyright law of 1891 and desperate for uncopyrighted books that would allow them to forgo royalty payments, rushed to publish *Black Rock*. *Westminster Magazine* had not copyrighted the chapters of the book when they first appeared in serial magazine form—the same mistake made with *In His Steps*—so even though Westminster published the book in Canada and Fleming H. Revell subsequently published it in the United States, the book was not protected by copyright. Eleven pirated editions priced from a quarter to a dollar soon appeared, encouraged in part by the St. Louis *Globe-Democrat*'s favorable review of the book (Mott 1947, 197).

Besides the promotional boost that *Black Rock* received in the United States from publishing pirates, its popularity was made possible largely from the same theme that helped to make novels by Harold Bell Wright bestsellers: what F.W. Watt appropriately called "the western myth" (1959, 26-36). Like the United States at the turn of the century, Canada was experiencing the settlement of its frontier, the development of its industries, and the growth of its cities. The fact and the myth of the economic individualism of the nineteenth century was being challenged by the idea of social interdependence. According to Watt, most people did not understand that "the units in economic relations were no longer individuals, the employer and his employee, but combinations—corporations, trusts, mergers, unions, associations" (1959, 29). Gordon's novels largely ignored this change; the protagonists in Gordon's stories were strong individuals whose spontaneous deeds based on sympathy and self-sacrifice benefited everyone they contacted (French 1930, 78). They idealized a bygone, individualistic world view to which Gordon and his readers were bound by temperament and by religious faith. Thus it is likely that his numerous North American readers, both above and below the border, reinforced their deep belief in society as an aggregate of autonomous individuals and resisted the nascent myth of collectivism.

Gordon's preference for the myth of community as the sum of distinctive personalities is clear in *Black Rock*. The novel begins when Ralph Connor, the narrator who makes illustrations by order for the railroads, accompanies his college varsity rugby chum Leslie Graeme to Black Rock, a mining and lumber camp of 350 in the Selkirk Mountains of western Canada that Graeme oversees. There they find a missionary and a miner's widow combatting the local saloon by trying to reason with and distract its patrons. They help to form an anti-saloon league, then a Presbyterian church, and finally a community center, which replaces the saloon. In the end, the widow and missionary marry.

This novel's great sales indicate that the book reflected, reinforced, or articulated the belief system of a large number of American readers. For this reason, examining the content of the novel for its belief system will suggest a pattern of religious values that the readers found acceptable if not simply true.

Evil is manifest in *Black Rock*. It stems from selfish disregard for others. Evil is always a character flaw, never ascribed to a social system or organization. Individuals propagate evil, and evil causes individuals to suffer. Typically evil is not done with the intention to harm others; evil is done because others are not considered at all. Evil deeds occur when individuals seek uninhibited self-gratification.

The first explanation of evil in *Black Rock* is made by Mr. Craig, the Black Rock missionary, when he produces an advertisement for a traveling show, sponsored by Mike Slavin, the barkeep, featuring farce and cancan dancing, to be followed by food and drinks. The minister worried that many of the miners and lumberjacks of Black Rock, having just received their quarterly pay in cash, would get drunk and lose their hard-earned wages to the bar's festivities:

"Last Christmas this town was for two weeks, as one of the miners said, 'a little suburb of hell.' It was something too awful. And at the end of it all one young fellow was found dead in his shack, and twenty or more crawled back to the camps, leaving their three months' pay with Slavin and his suckers" (p. 35).

The problem with the men of Black Rock gambling and spending their money on alcohol was that it kept the men separated from their families:

"some of them have wives, most of them mothers and sisters, in the east or across the sea, for whose sake they are slaving here; the miners hoping to save enough to bring their families to this homeless place, the rest to make enough to go back with credit. Why, there's Nixon, miner, splendid chap; has been here for two years, and drawing the highest pay. Twice he has been in sight of his heaven, for he can't speak of his wife and babies without breaking up, and twice that slick son of the devil—that's Scripture, mind you—Slavin, got him, and 'rolled' him, as the boys say. He went back to the mines broken in body and in heart. He says that this is his third and last chance. If Slavin gets him, his wife and babies will never see him on earth or in heaven" (pp. 36-37).

With only money in mind, Slavin sold liquor to men whose drinking caused deadly brawls and whose lavish bar tabs prevented them from rejoining their wives and children.

The choice of the name "Slavin" for the antagonist is revealing. The bondage that the name denotes is a sort of solitary confinement. Slavin is an individual who tempts others into immediate self-indulgence with utter disregard for one's relationships and responsibilities, or even for one's own long-term self-interest. Not only can a person become a slave to alcohol or gambling, but, more fundamentally, a person can become a slave to self-gratification. Such a person can have cohorts, but never a nurturing family.

Mike Slavin may be the major evil figure in *Black Rock*, but he has company in Idaho Jack, who spends his time at Slavin's to get drunk and to gamble. He is a violent and lawless hedonist, kept in line only by a 6'3" Mountie named Stonewall Jackson.

Idaho Jack is introduced in the novel in Slavin's saloon gambling with his gun on the table beside him: "He was shocked and disgusted when he discovered that a 'gun' was decreed by British law to be an unnecessary adornment of a card table" (pp. 158-59). When Stonewall Jackson confiscates the gun, Idaho Jack became "quite unable to play any more that evening, and it took several drinks all round to restore him to articulate speech" (p. 160). Idaho Jack buys another gun, but keeps it concealed.

His violence is illustrated in a scene where two members of the anti-saloon league are in the process of destroying kegs of Slavin's liquor. Idaho Jack draws a long knife to kill them. He fails, but not before breaking one of the men's wrists, and not before acknowledging that he was responsible for the death of his daughter as well as other people. Idaho Jack's anarchy and deathly violence are extensions of Slavin's selfishness. Both men cause suffering and death, the only difference being that Idaho Jack's link to the misery of others is more obvious and immediate.

Evil as selfish disregard for others appears in another, more subtle manner as well. It appears in religious intolerance, which is viewed as destructive of community. Dogmatism does not cause the pain of separation and death that the whiskey selling, gambling, and fighting of Idaho Jack and Slavin do, but it threatens to divide the religious community and so render it unable to combat the manifest evil in Black Rock. Because dogmatism divides community, it is attacked with like fervor.

Selfish disregard for others has one central source: the individual human will. The will itself is neither good nor bad, but it is a moral agent and as such takes on good or bad qualities whenever it acts. In *Black Rock*, an evil will is marked either by greed, in which case it actively promulgates evil, or by impotence, in which case it allows evil to flourish because it refuses to resist. In Roman Catholic parlance, the evil will is one which habitually commits sins of commission or sins of omission. Seen this way, the antagonist's name, Slavin, has significance because he is a slave to his greed and because he enslaves others by their inability to resist. *Black Rock* is a temperance novel which does not address the manufacture of liquor, but always the manufacturer; the distribution of liquor, but always the distributor; or the consumption of liquor, but always the consumer. Evil is individual, and though it takes an exterior form, it springs from one internal source: the individual will gone awry.

An individual who drinks liquor impairs his judgment and is likely to become an unwitting killer. The first episode of lethal drunkenness in *Black Rock* unfolds when the narrator learns why Mrs. Mavor is a widow. She had accompanied her husband Lewis to Black Rock because he had been hired to manage the miners. But Lewis lost his job because of his alcoholism, so he opened a hardware shop, continuing to drink until his daughter was born. For the next year and a half Lewis abstained from drinking, and his newfound sobriety led to the regained confidence of the mining company. One day, when his daughter was eighteen months old, Lewis was supervising the mining of a new drift. The two miners with him, however, had been drinking whiskey and accidentally set off an explosion, killing themselves as well as Mrs. Mavor's sober husband.

This scenario is played out more than once in *Black Rock*. Billy Breen, a drunkard reformed under the tender but firm care of the widowed Mrs. Mavor, drinks some lemonade that Slavin had spiked in order to regain his reformed customer. Under the influence, Billy goes to his shack, where he is found later "breathing heavily, covered up in his filthy, mouldering bed-clothes, with a half-empty bottle of whisky at his side" (p. 191). That was to be his last debauch. His heart failed the following day, and he was buried beside Lewis Mavor.

Another death by alcohol occurs shortly after Billy's burial. Geordie tells Slavin that Billy's "bluid is upon yer han's" and that "the Lord will require it o' you and yer hoose" (p. 205). Slavin's infant son becomes dangerously ill, and the doctor, habitually drunk on Slavin's whiskey, overdoses the baby, who convulses, falls asleep, and then dies. The evening of the child's death, the drunken doctor appears at Slavin's house and says, "Awfully sorry to hear of your loss, Mrs. Slavin; did our best you know, can't help this sort of thing" (p. 216).

The ostensible culprit in these three deaths is alcohol, but the narrative fixes the blame squarely on the individuals who sold or drank the liquor. Lewis Mavor died because "two men, half drunk with Slavin's whisky, set off a shot prematurely" (p. 91). When Billy is on his deathbed, he admits his own guilt, even though his first drink had not been his fault: "Oi haught t'a done better.

Oi 'm hawful sorry oi went back on 'im" (p. 192). Likewise, Slavin attempts to strangle the doctor, who he blames for the death of his son. However, in an exchange with a priest, he draws a different conclusion:

> "He murdered my child," growled Slavin.
> "Ah! how?"
> "He was drunk and poisoned him."
> "Ah! who gave him drink? Who made him a drunkard two years ago? Who has wrecked his life?"
> There was no answer, and the even-toned voice went relentlessly on—
> "Who is the murderer of your child now?"
> Slavin groaned and shuttered.
> "Go!" and the voice grew stern. "Repent of your sin and add not another" (p. 218).

Culpability is individual in these cases; death results when men lack the will to resist the lure of whiskey
 Billy, the doctor, and the two men who killed Mavor are willing dupes whose crime is more a lack of self control and shortsightedness than bad intent. But Slaving and Idaho Jack are conscious evil doers, reckless and impenitent. Slavin is greedy, and his sole concern is to get the Black Rock miners and lumberjacks to buy his liquor, despite the consequences of drinking. Although it is always people "drunk on Slavin's whiskey" who kill, Slavin is remorseless; only the sale counts for Slavin. Graeme, the director of mining at Black Rock, accuses Slavin of plying miners with liquor in order to rob them: "It is not the first time my men have lost money in the saloon" (p. 62). After Slavin and Idaho Jack spiked the lemonade that Billy Breen drank in good faith, Billy bought a bottle of whiskey and died. And Idaho, in order to win a $100 bet with Slavin, coerces Nixon into drinking:

The night was cold, and poor Nixon sat shivering on the edge of his bed. If he would take one drink they would leave him alone. He need not show himself so stiff. The whisky fumes filled his nostrils. If one drink would get them off, surely that was better than fighting and killing some one or getting killed. They sat about him amiably drinking, and lauding him as a fine fellow after all. One more glass before they left. Then Nixon rose, dressed himself, drank all that was left in the bottle, put his money in his pocket, and came down to the dance, wild with his old-time madness, reckless of faith and pledge,

forgetful of home, wife, babies, his whole being absorbed in one great passion—
to drink and drink and drink till he could drink no more (pp. 173-74).

Evil has two faces in *Black Rock*. One is malicious; the other
is unwitting. But whether by habit or occasion, both disregard others
in search of pleasure, pleasure found in the selling or drinking
of liquor. Both faces of evil are individual, and located in the
motivation and character of the will.

The ultimate source of deliverance from evil, which in *Black
Rock* stems from individuals' moral autism, is providence. God
is the author of goodness, of redirection, of changed motivation
and behavior. But even though conversion is attributed to providence
throughout the novel, God's participation in human affairs is
indirect and unclear. There is no *deus ex machina* in *Black Rock*,
no divine commands, no otherworldly manipulation of character
or action. God, that is to say, is the source of attribution for self-
improvement, but there is no evidence of God's direct participation
in human affairs.

God permeates *Black Rock*. In the first chapter, Jesus the Savior
is introduced in a blessing of the Christmas dinner by Mr. Craig,
the minister: "For Christ the Lord who came to save us, for all
the love and goodness we have known, and for these Thy gifts
to us this Christmas night, our Father, make us thankful" (p. 18).
After the meal, the minister tells how, as a child, the Christmas
story had inspired him, but that he lost the inspiration while he
was in college where he learned that the Bible was a collection
of children's stories, useless in the world of adults. This loss of
faith robbed him of the moral stamina needed to survive financial
hardship, so that he eventually found himself living a life of despair
and immorality in the slums. On Christmas, however, he heard
the Christmas story told in an inner city mission. He blurted out,
"Oh! can He save me?" and a young man responded, "Why! you
just bet He can!" Craig said, "I held to that hope with all my
soul, and...He hasn't failed me yet; not once, not once!" (p. 25).
In his prayer and his testimony, Craig attributed salvation to Christ,
but the only clue that he offered to the efficacy of salvation was
that his *embracing* the hope changed his life. The *source* of the
hope seems to have had little to do with the change.

The theme of providential deliverance from evil occurs again
and again in the novel. One Christmas Day, the veteran lumberjack
Nelson, "a man with his last chance before him" (p. 27), tells the

minister that as an old man, he has little to hope for. Mr. Craig, however, assures him that he can still be an agent of God's deliverance from evil. "He hasn't let go His grip of you," Craig says (p. 43). Immediately Nelson discovers his mission: to guard Sandy against the temptation of liquor, a temptation Sandy was too weak to resist alone. Again, God is the ultimate source of deliverance, but the immediate source of deliverance is human.

This theme is reiterated in the very title of the third chapter: "Waterloo. Our Fight—His Victory." The minister has organized an alternative to the festivities at Slavin's saloon: sports, followed by a Punch and Judy show (a famous English puppet play), culminating in a church meeting, where Mrs. Mavor sings. Drunken men from the saloon try to disrupt the sober meeting, but they are thwarted when Mrs. Mavor begins her heartfelt, inspired singing. Afterwards, the minister tells the gathering that Mrs. Mavor sang "because her heart is His who came to earth this day so many years ago to save us all; and she would make you love him too. For in loving Him you are saved from all base loves, and you know what I mean" (p. 74). Before he dismisses the audience, Mr. Craig asks for volunteers to resist the demon alcohol and to help their fellowmen do the same. A hundred men immediately volunteer by vowing in unison, "By God's help I will" (p. 75). The crux of deliverance from evil is God, the invisible partner in human resolve.

God is still mentioned after the hundred anti-saloon pledges are made. Billy, who is the most vulnerable of all the pledgers, falters, and Mrs. Mavor says to him, "Come, Billy there's no fear...God will help you" (p. 118). Shortly thereafter some men were studying the story of the Prodigal Son, and Nelson says a prayer: "Oh, Jesus Christ...we are a poor lot, and I'm the worst of the lot, and we are trying to find the way. Show us how to get back" (p. 144). Indeed, God's deliverance is spelled out as clearly as it is anywhere in the person of Nelson. Nelson, says Connor, "grew eager as he told how he had been helped, and how the world was all different, and his heart seemed new. He spoke of his Friend as if He were some one that could be seen out at camp, that he knew well, and met every day" (p. 152). God delivers people from evil by private, individual regeneration.

Final deliverance in *Black Rock* takes place when the saloon is converted into "a thoroughly equipped and well-conducted coffee-room, reading room, and hall" (p. 200), with travelling entertainers hired from time to time. This is planned, but the league must await the coming of a resident manager to operate it. Says Connor, "And come he did; but the manner of his coming was so extraordinary that I have believed in the doctrine of a special providence ever since" (pp. 202-203). The resident manager is to be the converted Slavin. After the death of his son, Slavin abandons his saloon and goes to work in the mines. By the end of three weeks, the league purchases and remodels the saloon and hires Slavin to manage it. On opening night, Slavin tells the clientele, "It's spacheless I am entirely. What's come to me I know not, nor how it's come. But I'll do my best for yez" (p. 223). Conversion is mysterious, divine, personal, and individual.

The human face of providential deliverance is the good will of individuals. Mr. Craig is a minister with a mission—to help the miners of Black Rock. Mrs. Mavor, who never experienced personal depravity, is equal in her resolve to care for the miners. Nelson converts as an old man, but he becomes as stalwart as the others in his drive to clean up Black Rock. So it is with all of the changed individuals in Black Rock. They attribute their strength of will to God, but their strength of will appears to be the result of human character become purposive. Deliverance in this sense is human. God receives the honors, but individuals muster their own resolve to help others. The reorientation from willful disregard for others to goodwill comes when individuals experience the results of others' self-regard and come to desire acts and attitudes of beneficence. This desire is the wellspring of deliverance from evil.

As the source of deliverance has two elements, providence and individual resolve, so also is the nature of the resolution two-fold. First is self-mastery, which means control of one's desires and the ability to withstand external temptations, particularly liquor and social pressure. Self-mastery, however, does not stand alone. It is always seen in relation to community, whether family or township. The dual virtues of empathy and forgiveness link self-mastery to community, so that the novel suggests that individual strength is never achieved in isolation, but always in the context of family and community.

That self-mastery is an essential characteristic of human fulfillment is clear form the beginning of *Black Rock*. In the first chapter, after the minister has told the men that he sank to the depths of depravity because "I began to lose my grip on myself," he makes this appeal to the men: "Without Him you'll never be the men you want to be, and you'll never get the better of that that's keeping some of you now from going back home" (p. 26). Self-mastery is both the personal goal and the personal means to family participation.

Later, when several men discuss the parable of the Prodigal Son, Baptiste asks, "How do you go back? You go to de pries'?" "The book doesn't say priest or any one else," said Nelson. "You go back in yourself, you see?" (p. 143) The minister's testimony is a personal appeal for self-mastery; this passage is a biblical appeal for the same end.

Most of the novel tells how men learn self-mastery in terms of abstinence from alcohol, but self-mastery is also illustrated in the context of romance and duty. By the time that Slavin reforms and becomes Resident Manager of the league's community center, the minister and the town widow are in love. No Black Rock marriage takes place, however, because both Mr. Craig and Mrs. Mavor have a higher duty. Craig must continue his frontier ministry, while Mrs. Mavor must go to England to care for her recently widowed mother-in-law and to supervise the Mavor estates. Mr. Craig and Mrs. Mavor falter, but their self-discipline sees them through. "One cannot shift one's responsibilities," says Mr. Craig, adding, "The only question is where your work lies" (p. 233). A few minutes later, he confesses to Mrs. Mavor his weakness for her: "Do not make me forget myself. You do not guess what you are doing" (p. 236).

Connor is outraged at duty triumphing over romance, but Graeme says, "I should not like to see him weaken" (p. 249). The value of self-mastery is made explicit when Graeme says, "Connor, that is great, to conquer oneself" (p. 253).

Because marriage and self-mastery are both valued highly in this novel, the two cannot ultimately be in conflict. The minister stays on with the mission while Mrs. Mavor does good works in England. Within two years, Mrs. Mavor's mother-in-law dies and she has to sell the estate to settle some debts—providence at work, no doubt—so she is free to return to Canada to care for Mr. Craig, who is recuperating from Rocky Mountain fever. They marry and return to the frontier to continue doing good works together.

Self-mastery is always seen as a value in light of the broader community. The major reason for miners to resist alcohol is family. Drinking miners squander their pay, so they cannot send financial support to their wives and children, nor can they earn enough money to be able to afford to return to live with their families.

Restraint is also necessary for the well-being of the frontier community itself. Drunken miners are deadly miners, and the deaths that they cause are always the deaths of others. Old Nelson, for instance, gained the resolve to stop drinking, and when Black Rock was disbanded, he was going home to his family. But he arrived in a coffin because Graeme, his companion, had been drinking and gambling in a San Francisco bar and had provoked a fight with a cheating card shark. The cheater drew a gun on Graeme, but Nelson protected him and died as a result. The focus in that episode is more on heroism than alcohol, but it is significant that Graeme felt guilty enough to vow never to drink again. Had he exercised self-control, they would not have been in the bar in the first place, and Nelson would have lived.

Community as the complement to self-mastery comes into focus with the efforts to found an anti-saloon league. Individualism is a limited value because no one can survive by means of individual resolve alone. Self-mastery can be maintained only through community support. In his appeal for the league, Craig says,

"Will the strong men help? Shall we all join hands in this? What do you say? In this town we have often seen hell, and just a moment ago we were all looking into heaven, 'the sweet and blessed country.'... Oh men! which shall be ours? For Heaven's dear sake, let us help one another" (p. 75).

During the meeting in which the league was formed, a miner made a similar appeal for group support:

He had come to this country to make his fortune; now he was anxious to make enough to enable him to go home with some degree of honour. His home held everything that was dear to him. Between him and that home, between him and all that was good and beautiful and honourable, stood whisky. "I am ashamed to confess...that I feel the need of some such league" (pp. 106-107).

Self-mastery, then, is not an end in itself. It is an essential good, but it is incomplete, if not impossible, without community support. Community, however, is not merely a means for attaining self-mastery; it is also the reason for attaining self-mastery. There is no narcissism in self-control. In this sense, community is a more fundamental value than individuality, but the individual is by no means consumed by community. The nature of resolution in *Black Rock* is self-mastery in concert with, and because of, community.

In *Black Rock*, the method of attaining resolution closely resembles the nature of the resolution itself: It involves individual resolve in concert with community support. God's providence is always in the background, but good human action is emphasized. The theology here is not one of grace—the unmerited favor that human beings receive from God—but rather one of works, both individual and corporate. God may orchestrate deliverance, but individuals perpetrate it.

Resolution is attained in two interlocking steps. The first step is to gain individual resolve, which is tantamount to gaining religious faith. Craig gains the moral courage to abstain from alcohol in an inner city mission where he learns that God will save and sustain him. Nelson takes his vow of abstinence from alcohol when he finds the faith to believe in God as his eternal friend and supporter. Billy signs the anti-drinking pledge when he comes to believe that despite his history of alcoholism, God still accepts him and will help him lead a sober life. Slavin destroys the stock of liquor in his saloon and gains the determination to fight liquor when a priest blames him for his child's death and admonishes him, "Repent of your sin and add not another" (p. 218). Graeme gains the resolve to quit drinking and simultaneously develops faith. He tells a doubting, drinking friend:

"I haven't much of a creed...don't really know how much I believe. But...I do know that good is good, and bad is bad, and good and bad are not the same. And I know a man's a fool to follow the one, and a wise man to follow the other, and...I believe God is at the back of a man who wants to get done with bad" (p. 294).

Faith accompanies moral resolve in *Black Rock*, but faith, like moral resolve, is more of an individual achievement than a gift of grace.

The complement of individual resolve in achieving resolution is community support. No one fights the demon alcohol alone. Even in the beginning of the novel when the minister appears to be a solitary voice in the wilderness, it is a duet with the widow that the camp hears. Mr. Craig preaches and Mrs. Mavor sings.

The first call for abstinence is given at a public meeting, with volunteers for mutual support being solicited: "For Heaven's dear sake, let us help one another!" (p. 75). That appeal wins a hundred volunteers. The volunteers then meet to decide whether the anti-saloon league would abstain from alcohol or drink only in moderation. Nixon summarizes the feelings of the men: "The only way to stop its work is to quit drinkin' it and help others to quit" (p. 106). When the league meets to form Black Rock Presbyterian Church, 38 people sign the charter, forming a core of faithful whiskey fighters. The reformed drinkers do help one another abstain, and they also fight the saloon *en masse* by breaking into the saloon to destroy kegs of liquor and by sponsoring an alcohol-free ball as an alternative to entertainment in the saloon. Finally, alcohol is beaten in Black Rock when the league establishes a community entertainment center and recruits the newly reformed Slavin to manage it.

The power of community is not simply its numbers, although quantity does figure largely in the notion of community support. Rather, community is marked by certain characteristics which make it effective. Preeminent is open-mindedness, which recognizes and appreciates individuality within the goal-sharing community. According to the narrator, Black Rock "possessed in a marked degree that eminent Christian virtue of tolerance. All creeds, all shades of religious opinion, were allowed, and it was generally conceded that one was as good as another" (p. 121). Variety is respected because it results from individuals grappling with shared concerns. "The Black Rock varieties of religion were certainly startling; but there was undoubtedly the streak of reality though them all, and that discovery I felt to be a distinct gain," says the narrator (p. 136). Near the end of novel, Connor meets up with Craig, who has spent a year's leave of absence in Edinburgh. He describes the minister's increased depth in terms of open-mindedness: "He was more tolerant of opinions other than his own, but more unrelenting in his fidelity to conscience and more impatient of half-heartedness and self-indulgence" (p. 310). Here the link between self-mastery, moral resolve, and open-mindedness—three of the cardinal virtues in *Black Rock*—is made explicit.

Besides tolerance, the mark of communal spirit is forgiveness. When Billie, who had vowed never to drink again, unknowingly drinks spiked lemonade, he becomes fatally ill. But before he dies, he tells Mrs. Mavor, "Hit was the lemonade. The boys didn't mean no 'arm—but hit started the 'ell hinside." Then he says, "Don't be 'ard on 'em Geordie; they didn't mean no 'arm" (p. 192). Likewise the league forgives Slavin, whose whiskey had caused much of the suffering in Black Rock, and demonstrates its forgiveness by hiring him to manage the community center. Late in the novel, when Graeme confesses his inadvertent role in the death of Nelson, he asks Nelson's daughter, "Can you forgive me? I brought him to his death." She replies, "You would have done the same for him" (p. 272). Forgiveness is tolerance put to the test, and both characterize that type of community which, with the power of individual resolve, can overcome the problems of selfish disregard for others.

The belief system in *Black Rock* reflects or reinforces certain chief values among the readers. It affirms the traditional Christian church and the belief in God as omnipresent. It also affirms the values of individualism, family, and community. Individuals count in *Black Rock*, but they are always seen as incomplete without their nuclear family or their immediate community. There is also an implied equality here, so that each person, regardless of class, church, or ethnic background is as good as another. The world in Black Rock, that is to say, is an orderly Christian democracy. Social structure and power and the secular state are disregarded in favor of faith in individual self-determination and family or community support.

After Black Rock

Between the publication of *Black Rock* and the outbreak of World War I, Gordon was busy writing novels—*Black Rock: A Tale of the Selkirks* (1898), *The Sky Pilot: A Tale of the Foothills* (1899), and *The Man from Glengarry: A Tale of the Ottawa* (1901) are considered to be his best[2]—getting married, and continuing his education. Gordon produced manuscripts annually for the Christmas market, but rarely on schedule. His editor in the United States, George H. Doran, described Gordon's tardiness:

The beginning of each year we would make a contract for a manuscript to be delivered by July, for his readers wanted a new book by Christmas. July would come and go with only a portion of the manuscript in hand. Finally it became a recognized procedure for me to get him to Chicago, and later to New York, and literally put him under lock and key until the manuscript was completed.... We never failed to publish one of his books in the late autumn of the season for which it was intended even though the date would be November 25 instead of October 15, and we would be obliged to cable the last hundred thousand words to London for the British edition (Doran 1952, 203).

In 1904, Gordon was elected a fellow of the elite academic fraternity, the Royal Society of Canada, and two years later he received a Doctor of Divinity degree from Knox College. When Canada was called to arms, the sixty-year-old Gordon became the chaplain of the 79th Cameron Highlanders of Canada. Because Canada had no draft, Gordon toured the country making appeals for swift and massive enlistments. He requested that he accompany his regiment overseas, so he was in England as the 79th arrived, having been appointed chief chaplain of the Canadian forces in England as a major. When the Canadian forces were sent on active duty to France, Gordon resigned his commission as chief chaplain of the Canadian forces in England and went with them as the senior chaplain of the 3rd Division of France. Shortly thereafter, in 1917, the British government sent him from France to encourage the United States to end its three-year neutrality and join the Allies. He made a number of public appearances and even met privately with President Wilson, who assured him that "something will happen shortly."

Before leaving for Britain, Gordon made sure that his wife and children—six girls and one boy—would receive $100 thousand each upon his death, the sum being what Gordon had made through keen investments of his royalties. Near the end of the war, however, Gordon was shocked to learn that not only was he not the near-millionaire he had been led to believe he was, but that he was almost $100 thousand in debt. One of the soldiers in Gordon's outfit, Colonel Thompson, a lawyer from Winnipeg who had been in charge of Gordon's investments, had mismanaged Gordon's finances. Thompson had invested Gordon's money in real estate outside Winnipeg, believing that Winnipeg would become Canada's Chicago, and even when land values dropped in 1913, Thompson continued to assure Gordon that his investments were solid. Gordon made this discovery only after Thompson had died in battle in France. Gordon spent years settling the debts his friend had incurred, only to have the City of Winnipeg take over his house for taxes after he died (Doran 1952, 205).

After the war, Gordon returned to Canada where he continued to write and to serve the Presbyterian Church. Between 1920 and 1924, he chaired the Joint Council of Industry for the Province of Manitoba, which settled over one hundred labor disputes following the Winnipeg General Strike of 1919. During this period he also served as moderator of the Presbyterian Church, and he was instrumental in the 1924 merger of the Presbyterian, Congregational, and Methodist Churches, forming the United Church of Canada. In 1932, Woodrow Wilson asked him to deliver the opening address to the League of Nations. Gordon died on October 31, 1937 in Winnipeg (Grant 1983, 306).

Popularity

Gordon's popularity in the United States is evident not only from *Black Rock*'s phenomenal sales—more copies sold south of the border than in his native Canada—but also from his personal reception in the United States. Police were called to control American crowds when he spoke. Henry Ford, as he hosted Gordon for lunch, presented him with a stack of Gordon's novels for him to autograph, and a Detroit congregation to whom Gordon was speaking interrupted a prayer by singing "For He's a Jolly Good Fellow" (Paterson 1953, 26).

Gordon believed that his popularity was the result of three factors. First was the religious message of the novels. Religion is central to human being, Gordon believed, so it is obvious why his novels would have a wide appeal:

Religion is here set forth in its true light as a synonym of all that is virile, straight, honorable and withal tender and gentle in true men and women. And it was this religious motif that startled that vast host of religious folk who up to this time had regarded novel-reading as a doubtful indulgence for Christian people. I have received hundreds of letters expressing gratitude for a novel that presented a quality of religious life that "red-blooded men could read and enjoy" (Gordon 1938, 150).

The *Reader Magazine* agreed:

"In a time when nine hundred and ninety-nine out of every thousand books are avowedly secular in their tone, the devotional quality of his stories brings comfort and satisfaction to thousands who desire to see in fiction, as they do in the lives about them, evidences of the living observance of the Christian faith" (1904, 105).

Gordon's novels like *Black Rock* may contain a religious belief system, but they ignore certain central religious themes. Doran called Gordon's novels "red-blooded thrillers" that upheld "a real religion of reverence and common sense" (1952, 206). Gordon did raise the question of why God permits humans to suffer in *The Sky Pilot*— pain is a divine instrument for human improvement, so the novel suggests—but he typically bypassed theological questions in favor of moral ones. Although an early issue of *Book News* declared that Gordon had "that spiritual touch, all his own, so rare, subtle, sure" (1901, 355), Leclerc is much more accurate in saying, "Charles Gordon very seldom refers to grace and the real power of prayer. For him, good example and powerful preaching are the main elements in the conversion of even the most hardened sinners who may change completely in a remarkably short time" (1962, 67). As Watt points out, Gordon's God of the west is generous, relatively tolerant, and unprejudiced (1969, 33). Like the other bestsellers in this study, *Black Rock* focuses more on Christian *morality* than on *Christian* morality. And the term "Christian" is an ambiguous qualifier. For Gordon, there are good guys and bad guys, the distinction being neighborliness and care for their families, and good women—always good women (based on his memory of his mother, who died in 1890, when Gordon was thirty years old). In this sense, *Black Rock* can be understood as a Victorian morality tale told in religious terms.

Gordon also thought that his popularity was due in part to his craftsmanship in that the characters came to life for the readers who wanted to read realistic prose. But as with most popular writers, particularly those who write social melodrama, Gordon has been criticized for his emotional and intellectual sloppiness, "emotional exuberances," as the review of *Black Rock* in *The Spectator* labeled it (1899, 58). Even Lionel Leclerc, who generally flatters the Ralph Connor books, laments what he calls the "agonizing sentimental-ity," saying that Gordon sometimes "loses all sense of proportion and abandons himself to a shameless wallowing in emotion" (1962, 83). In his description of Gordon's novels' characteristics, Leclerc rehearses the familiar litany of complaints about social melodramas:

His characters are stereotyped—the hard-working mother forever ready to help everyone, the strong, silent man with a heart of gold, and the ruffian. The good characters are completely static while the less desirable specimens of humanity are susceptible to incredibly swift conversions. As for the plots, there is little regard for probability, as evidenced by series of melodramatic incidents or coincidences (1961, 32).

Perhaps Gordon's lack of stylistic flair results from his purposiveness. The *Christian Century* supported Robert Haddow's earlier declaration that Gordon's writings and his work as a minister are inseparable (1899, 700) by saying,

> He never was, never tried to be, a great novelist. But he could write a strong, swift moving story and make it carry a message of moral idealism and practical Christianity.... If anyone ever told him his novels were "preaching," he was doubtless glad to hear it. They were good preaching (1937, 1381).

According to Watt, however, Gordon's moralism did not cause his prose misdemeanors; in fact, Gordon sank as a novelist when he began to conceive of himself more as a novelist who was also a preacher than as a preacher who was also a novelist. "The later novels," writes Watt, "in which Connor is very rarely the preacher, are his most unconvincing and trivial" (1959, 35). Perhaps the truth is that Gordon attracted hoards of readers at the time when they wanted to hear his message of rugged but charitable individualism on the frontier, but that he did not have the mimetic skills to succeed as a writer of non-formula fiction, nor did he have another message to succeed as a social melodramatist when the audience's agenda had changed. Gordon, that is, was a single-formula, single-theme writer:

> The bulk of Connor's novels adhered to a single and highly successful formula— the playing out of a morality in a magnificent natural setting, with colourful characterizations and vivid descriptive passages to put flesh on the archetypal confrontation of men with their unruly souls (Thompson and Thompson 1972, 159).

The reading public wanted that formula for a short time, but the interest was ephemeral. By the 1920s, Gordon's popularity had waned: "The postwar generation was disenchanted and its disenchantment had no room for an optimistic belief in moral regeneration" (Paterson 1953, 60).

But more attractive than the religion or the verisimilitude of his novels to Gordon was the power inherent in the landscape of the west. His U.S. editor, George H. Doran, put it simply: "He wrote of the West at a time when Western stories were in great demand the world over" (1952, 205). Leclerc attributes Gordon's popularity to a very large readership interested in the vanishing frontier: "Ralph Connor came just when readers were ready for the type of books which brought them in contact with a brand-new country being opened by brave and enterprising men and women whose deeds stirred the imagination" (1962, 90). As the frontier closed, people idealized a world of rugged mountains and open plains and the free-spirited Indians, Mounties, and miners who raised their families and overcame the elements together. Besides a rose-colored vision of the frontier, readers also wanted the vicarious violence that books like Gordon's offered. According to Leclerc, "Connor's books had the same kind of appeal as our own hockey matches or boxing bouts where the reader gets vicarious thrills without the danger of injury" (1962, 69).

Gordon believed that the frontier controlled his creativity. Certainly it was the raison d'être of *Black Rock,* in terms of motivation, text, and sales. At the time Gordon's social consciousness was developing, he and his readers accepted the myth of individualism that underlies *Black Rock.* As Gordon's social consciousness matured—as evident in his involvement with labor arbitration, church union, and the League of Nations—his readership declined. Apparently Gordon's work with collectives cost him broad public appeal. Gordon outgrew the "Ralph Connor" of *Black Rock,* and the gains he made in social work were lost on his readership.

Chapter Four

Harold Bell Wright's Laws of Nature

During the first two decades of the twentieth century, the novels of Harold Bell Wright outsold those of any other writer, religious or otherwise. Like both Sheldon and Gordon, Wright was a preacher whose bestsellers were fictional sermons that captured the imagination of the American reading public. No matter that few know of Wright today or that even fewer still read his books; Wright signified what a great number of early twentieth-century Americans believed or wanted to believe. Wright's books, that is to say, are nothing short of cultural phenomena, and as such can reveal a major strain of pre-World War I American values.

Wright's popularity is clear both from sales figures and contemporary reports. Wright produced five bestsellers, according to Frank Luther Mott's stringent criterion that a bestseller sell at least as many copies as one per cent of the U.S. population for the decade in which it was published (1947, 303). These books were *The Shepherd of the Hills* (1907), 1.2 million copies; *The Calling of Dan Matthews* (1909), 925 thousand copies; *The Winning of Barbara Worth* (1911), 900 thousand copies; *The Eyes of the World* (1914), 925 thousand copies; and *When a Man's a Man* (1916), 965 thousand copies. A woman who ran a canteen, which had a small library, in France during World War I, recalled:

But though practically everything in the nature of a novel or story went well, I soon came to know that ten out of a dozen of the boys who asked for a book would say first:
  "Got anything by Harold Bell Wright?"
  If I had they took it. If I had not, they took anything else. It was Harold Bell Wright against the field, with Wright winning every time. There were only four of his books in my library, and they were on the go unceasingly....

And not only the doughboy—the officers, when they dropped in to see if there was something to read, usually made the same request (Hawthorne 1923b, 104-105; Hawthorne 1923a, 6-7; Farrar 1925, 661).

She added, "If you want to know America in the bulk read one of Wright's books, and try to get back of it to the men and women who ask for him in the millions, who want him because he expresses what they need to have expressed" (p. 112).

Grant C. Knight observed that Wright was "one of the most read and most ridiculed writers of his generation" (1954, 129). His popularity particularly perplexed writers in *The Bookman*, who landed on sentimentality as the key to Wright's popularity (Cooper 1915; Phelps 1921). In a review of *The Calling of Dan Matthews*, Frederic Cooper said,

People who read books of this type are not looking for high artistic quality; they are looking chiefly for certain types of distinctly American character, depicted with a certain graphic accuracy; a moderate quantity of more or less whimsical humor and an underlying strain of religious sentiment which sometimes verges on sentimentality (1909, 189).

Two years later, *The Bookman's* review of *The Winning of Barbara Worth* called sentimentality "a vice which infects the very fibre of Mr. Wright's mental fabric and which, constituting no doubt, a prime virtue for his admirers, goes far toward explaining his popular success as a novelist" (Bradley 1911, 98). The critics' disdain is even clearer in an April 1924 *Literary Review* essay which began, "There is a richness in social satire...in the works of Harold Bell Wright," and ended, "April Fool!" (Tutler 1924, 645). Wright's novels, particularly *When a Man's a Man*, became the subject of parodies, as in Donald Ogden Stewart's "How Love Came to General Grant" (1921) and Corey Ford's "When a Rollo Boy's a Rollo Boy or, Virtue Triumphant in Three Weeks" (1925) which highlighted Wright's plot manipulations and the happy endings that invariably included a marriage or engagement in the very last chapter.

Whether they shaped or reflected American values, Wright's bestsellers certainly embody the values of his readers who, in turn, represented a mainstream in the American culture (Nelson 1976, 20-21). The popularity of Wright's novels, bolstered by modern marketing techniques, was due primarily to his use of social melodrama, in which he romanticized the frontier past with a faith in unspoiled nature and a moral code of hard work, clean living, and neighborliness.

Wright Before Bestsellers

That Harold Bell Wright would become the bestselling writer of the early twentieth century appears to be fortuitous insofar as his education and family background are concerned. He was born on Spring Brook Farm near Rome, New York on 4 May 1872, the second of four sons, two of whom died in childhood. Wright's mother, the former Alma T. Watson, died when he was eleven years old. Her sole literary bequest, it appears, was the gift of her son's first book, Longfellow's *Hiawatha*. His father, William A. Wright, was a poor, alcoholic carpenter who had served as a lieutenant for the Union during the Civil War.

After his mother died, Wright was moved about New York state under the care of his father or other relatives. He first moved to Whitesboro, then to Sennett, where he stayed with an uncle. Afterwards he moved to an aunt's near Milan, Ohio and finally rejoined his father in Lima, Ohio and then in Findlay, Ohio. Wright's religious sensibilities were awakened in Findlay where he saw a production of Goethe's *Faust*:

I was witnessing the eternal clash of spiritual forces which in every soul makes for ultimate salvation or final destruction. It was to me a tremendous spiritual experience that shook my very being (Wright 1934, 114).

This religious awakening was nurtured when he attended a revival meeting conducted by a Hiram College senior. The young Disciples of Christ preacher convinced Wright to study for the ministry at the Ohio college.

Wright enrolled in the pre-preparatory department—the equivalent of junior high school today—at Hiram College in the fall of 1892. There he wrote his first story, "From an Indian Battle." He studied at Hiram College for two years, until eye trouble and pneumonia prevented him from working as a quarry- and factory-hand to pay for tuition (Patrick 1925). He left in 1894, never to continue his formal education.

For the next three years, Wright slowly made his way westward, earning his keep by doing farm work and painting landscapes on the sides of delivery wagons. He ended up in the Ozarks, where he began preaching:

Thanksgiving was to be observed in the White Oak district with an all-day meeting at the schoolhouse not far from my uncle's home. The neighbors would bring baskets of food and there would be a community Thanksgiving dinner. A preacher was coming to hold services.

At the last minute we learned that, for some reason, the preacher could not come.

A long, lean hill-billy approached me. "You got edication, mister, why can't you preach to we-uns?"

I answered impulsively, "I reckon I can" (Wright 1934, 200).

I thought...that I could do almost as well as a minister I had heard a few Sundays before, who announced as his text, "Ye are the salt of the earth, but if the salt has lost its Savior wherewith shall it be salted?" (Millard 1917, 464).

Wright continued to preach in the following weeks, and he was soon offered the pastorate at the Christian (Disciples) Church in Pierce City, Missouri for $400 per year (Reynolds 1916, 7). He served as pastor there from 1897 to 1898.

Wright left Pierce City to replace a minister in Pittsburg, Kansas who had been living under an assumed name. He preached there from 1898 until 1903. In 1899 he married Frances E. Long of Buffalo, New York, whom he had met in Hiram College. His first son, Gilbert Munger, was born in 1901, and his second, Paul Williams, followed the year after.

Wright's literary career began in Pittsburg. According to Wright:

My idea was to read this story to my congregation on the installment plan. No doubt I was influenced in this by Charles M. Sheldon and his book 'In His Steps.' Nothing could have been farther from my thoughts than that this story was to be the beginning of my work as a writer (1934, 211).

Doubtlessly Wright did envision an audience past the pews of the Disciples Church in Pittsburg, Kansas, an audience Wright sought during the winter of 1901-02 when he took several weeks' leave of absence to assist in a revival meeting in Chicago. One evening, after preaching a sermon entitled "Sculptors of Life," Wright met Elsbery W. Reynolds, owner of the Book Supply Company, a mail-order firm in Chicago. Wright and Reynolds became friends, and the two of them went over the manuscript of *That Printer of Udell's* and made some revisions. Reynolds published the book in 1903, with an initial printing of a thousand copies (Mott 1947, 228; Baxter 1970, 2). The Book Supply Company catalog contained an entire chapter from the novel, with full-page illustrations. Large orders of the novel soon followed ("Grief," 57-58). Eventually, 450 thousand copies of *That Printer of Udell's* were sold.

That Printer of Udell's concerned unemployment, alcoholism, class barriers, and crime, social problems which, according to the novel, were exacerbated if not caused by the social unconcern of creedal churches. The churches were not following the Sermon on the Mount, which meant that they did not know that steady work is more important than religious doctrines. "A feller's got to be a man before he can be much of a Christian" (p. 333), says one of the characters, and this principle is illustrated by the protagonist, a reformed drinker and hobo who finds a job, works hard and saves money, marries an upper-class Christian girl, becomes a believer himself, becomes a church leader, and finally is elected to the House of Representatives. Religion, in Wright's first book, concerns success which follows work in the here-and-now more than salvation which follows belief in the by-and-by. This theme pervades all of Wright's books.

The Shepherd of the Hills

After publishing *That Printer of Udell's*, Wright accepted a pastorate in Kansas City, where he preached from 1903 until 1905. His health failed, however, so he returned to the Ozarks for a pastorate in Lebanon, Missouri where he wrote his best-known book, *The Shepherd of the Hills*.

The Shepherd of the Hills is set in the Ozark Mountains of southwest Missouri. Daniel Howitt, a learned and cultured Chicago minister, arrives for no other apparent reason than to rest in the seclusion of Mutton Hollow. Although he keeps his background a secret, he is befriended by Grant Matthews, Sr., a farmer and miller whose only daughter died giving birth to a mystical boy named Pete. Matthews hires Howitt as a shepherd, and the minister quickly becomes the mentor to the two young adults of Mutton Hollow: Young Matt, the only surviving child of Grant Matthews, and Sammy Lane, Young Matt's lifelong companion. The novel concerns the temptations that these characters overcome.

One temptation concerns marriage. Nineteen-year-old Sammy Lane must choose whether to marry her fiancé, Ollie Stewart, who has left the hills for Kansas City to gain wealth and social position, or Young Matt, who is the biggest and strongest man in the backwoods and who is as good-hearted as he is powerful. Sammy asks "Dad" Howitt to teach her to be a lady so that she will be sophisticated enough to move to the city when her suitor returns for her. Howitt complies, but the more Sammy understands the great books of western civilization, the less taken she is with her fiancé and his city ways. When Ollie returns to the mountains, Sammy breaks their engagement. He promises her jewels and dresses, but she says,

I might, indeed, find many things in your world that would be delightful, but I fear that I should lose the things that after all are, to me, the really big things. I do not feel that the things that are greatest in your life could bring happiness without that which I find here. And there is something here that can bring happiness without what you call the advantages of the world to which you belong (p. 207).

Ollie returns to Kansas City, and Sammy waits for her true love, Young Matt, to propose.

Young Matt has his own temptation to overcome: whether to be controlled by brain or brawn. He is the strongest man in his part of the country. He can lift an iron grain mill, pick up two grown men by the belt, one in each hand, and thrust them over his head, and snap rope that binds his wrists behind his back. When used against evildoers—protecting Sammy from the bad intent of the county bully, Wash Gibbs, or breaking the arm of a ruffian who would knife him in the back—Young Matt's strength is virtuous. But he is tempted to let his emotions control his muscles. When he overhears two men ridiculing him at a dance, he approaches them, fists clenched, but he walks out the door instead. When he spots a panther about to pounce on Ollie Stewart, his enemy in romance, he hesitates for a moment before shoving the weakling aside to fight the deadly animal alone. Young Matt takes the shepherd's words to heart:

It is always a God's blessing, lad, when a man masters the worst of himself. You are a strong man, my boy. You hardly know your strength. But you need always to remember that the stronger the man, the easier it is for him to become a beast. Your manhood depends upon this, and upon nothing else, that you conquer and control the animal side of yourself (p. 172).

Young Matt does control his brawn, thus showing himself to be strong both in spirit and in body.

Young Matt's father faces a temptation similar to his son's. He is, after all, the source of his son's physical prowess. Grant Matthews must choose between understanding and revenge. When he first tells Howitt about his daughter's abandonment and death, he says, "Many's the time I have prayed all night that God would let me meet him again just once, or that proud father of his'n, just once, sir. I'd glad go to Hell if I could only meet them first" (p. 46). Grant's intent is obvious: "the giant's voice took a tone of terrible meaning.... [H]e was standing erect, his muscles tense, his powerful frame shaken with passion" (p. 46). Near the end of the novel, Howitt confesses to Grant that he is the father of the artist who left Grant's daughter to die in childbirth. Howitt has just discovered his son, who is dying after fifteen years of penitential hiding in a nearby cave. The son has asked to see Grant so that he can ask forgiveness. Howitt wonders, "Was the strong man's passion really tame? Or was his fury only sleeping, waiting to destroy the one who should wake it?" (p. 273) Grant does control his rage, even accompanying the shepherd to the hideout where he forgives the man who caused his only daughter to die. "It's sure God's way," he says to Howitt (p. 282).

The artist's apparent heartlessness had been largely due to his father's misbegotten pride. The son had fallen in love with the Matthews girl, but knowing that his highly educated, urban father would disapprove of his choice of an uneducated, rural mate, he abandoned her. He wrote her a letter explaining his decision to leave, as Grant Matthews recounts:

It told over and over how he loved her and how no woman could ever be to him what she was; said they was made for each other, and all that; and then it went on to say how he couldn't never see her again; and told about what a grand old family his was, and how his father was so proud and expected such great things from him, that he didn't dare tell, them bein' the last of this here old family, and her bein' a backwoods girl, without any schoolin' or nothin' (p. 44).

Because absence did not diminish his love, he returned for her, leaving a note for his father that suggested that he had committed suicide. By this time, however, she had borne a son and had died. That is when he holed up in a cave, taking care of his son Pete who was mystical by nature and allowed to run free.

Howitt went to the mountains to quell his grief. His faith was intellectual and unsustainable, so he escaped to the mountains for relief from emotional pressures, changing his name to make his escape effective. When Grant Matthews unknowingly tells him of his son's heartlessness, Howitt decides to stay in order to atone for the sin that resulted from his pride. He experiences forgiveness and is born again, so that he never again assumes his former identity. As he tells Grant, "I have no name but the name by which you know me. The man who bore that name is dead. In all his pride of intellect and position he died" (p. 279). Living in the mountains rejuvenated the weary minister both physically and spiritually, providing him with a new identity to accompany his altered name.

The Shepherd of the Hills harbors a suspicion of city life and glorifies a vision of rural wisdom, obvious responses to the burgeoning cities and vanishing frontiers of Wright's era. The appeal is melodramatic and popular, all the more revealing of certain middle-class values during the early twentieth-century. Although this novel does not propose a program of social salvation like *In His Steps* and *Black Rock* do, it resembles them in that it is a popular religious response to problems of the day. For this reason, the novel's belief system merits close attention.

In this novel, evil is materialism, or the lack of inwardness, of spirituality. Materialism is associated with death and pain on the one hand and with foolishness and cowardice on the other. Evil is common, in that everyone in the novel is at least lured by materialism, but few succumb. In other words, materialism is a menace that can be defeated.

The pathetic side of materialism is evident in the character of Ollie Stewart. Ollie dreams of managing his uncle's business in Kansas City, thus becoming a man of wealth and social position. When he returns from the city, he was a "slender, pale-faced man, with faultless linen, well-gloved hands and shining patent leathers" (p. 162). He compliments Sammy on her beauty, and then chides her for sounding uneducated. "If you talk like that in the city," he warns her, "people will know in a minute that you are from the country" (p. 163). When Sammy tries to discuss meaningful issues with him, he responds in clichés and flippant remarks. He does not tell Sammy about Young Matt's willingness to save him from the panther, and he stands by helplessly as Wash Gibbs threatens to molest his fiancée. Ollie, as the diminutive name suggests, is a cowardly, manipulative young man who attends to appearance without regard for human depth. The narrative dismisses his values as being "foam and froth" (p. 164).

Wash Gibbs carries materialism to the point of lawlessness. He will do anything to gratify his physical and material desires. He kills two men and nearly kills two others who he perceives as hindrances to his thievery. He robs a local bank of all its gold, and he persistently threatens to rape Sammy Lane. Gibbs is kept only partially in line by Sammy's gun-toting father and Young Matt's superior strength.

If the cravings of Ollie Stewart and Wash Gibbs represent the extremes of materialism—the lust for surface beauty and riches by tenderfoot and roughneck alike—then the temptations that the main characters face represent more common materialist desires. Young Matt and his father, for instance, must learn the practice of patience and thoughtfulness in order to control their reflex to pummel their problems away. They learn to hunt an interior, rather than an exterior, quarry. Sammy Lane almost marries a man in order to share the glitter of his status and wealth, but she comes to understand that real sophistication is more heart than plume. Finally, Dad Howitt, like his son, struggles to excise social acceptability from faith and love. Materialism is more than the desire for physical riches. It encompasses all that is valued that is not interior, spiritual, of the heart. Materialism not only mistakes the clothes for the man; it prefers the clothes to the man.

There is a sense of determinism, both biological and social, in *The Shepherd of the Hills* that goes far beyond the social influences that the other religious bestsellers of the era depict. The narrative repeatedly speaks of good blood, bad blood, old blood, and blue blood, as if a person's biological lineage has moral characteristics. The novel does not exactly preach eugenics, but from place to place it does advocate selective human breeding. If a person's biological heritage does not quite explain good and evil in this novel, then a person's habitat gives added insight. Wilderness is pitted against city, and although neither quite determines moral behavior, the novel suggests that urban life is oppressive and that rural life is liberating. Nature together with nurture create moral character, which is made certain by a small degree of free will.

The power of lineage is forthrightly expressed early in the novel. Preachin' Bill, a mountain sage who is quoted frequently, says,

Hit's a plumb shame there ain't more men in th' world built like old man
Matthews and that thar boy o' his'n. Men like them ought t' be as common
as th' other kind, an' would be, too, if folks cared half as much 'bout breeding
folks as they do 'bout raising hogs an' horses (p. 12).

This passage refers to both the physical and the moral qualities
of these two protagonists. Likewise, Sammy Lane is told, " 'You
got as good blood as the best of the thoroughbreds' " (p. 63). Her
father came from southern aristocracy, her mother from the Ozark
mountains: "in her veins there was mingled the blue blood of the
proud southerners and the warm red life of her wilderness mother"
(p. 64). When Gibbs says that he has been trying unsuccessfully
to get close to Sammy, her father tells him, "She's got mighty good
blood in her veins, that girl has; and I don't aim to ever let it
be mixed up with none of the low down common yeller kind"
(pp. 104-105). Ollie Stewart, Sammy's fiancé throughout most of
the book, has "pretty good" blood (p. 105), but it is impure, as
evidenced by his cowardice. "Bank on the old blood every time,"
Sammy's father says. "There ain't a drop of yeller in it; not a drop,
Sammy. Ollie ain't to say bad, but he ain't just our kind" (p. 204).
The only other reference to blood lines occurs at the end of the
novel in reference to Howitt: "it was due very largely, no doubt,
to the same ancestral influence that he became what the world calls
a successful minister of the gospel" (p. 275). This passage
summarizes the importance of breeding to moral character: breeding
is a major factor, but not the only one.

Social factors are less determinative. Howitt's son's heartless
abandonment of his lover is the result of the superficiality and
snobbishness of urban culture, the reason his father seeks redemption
in the mountains. City life, Howitt tells Mrs. Matthews, "demands
almost too much at times; I often wonder if it's worth the struggle"
(p. 27). As he looks at Mrs. Matthews' furrowed, kindly face, he
thinks of the contrast in women of the city, "women whose soft
hands knew no heavier task than the filmy fancy work they toyed
with, and whose greatest care, seemingly, was that time should leave
upon their faces no record of the passing years" (p. 28). Ollie is
much like these city women, worrying more about status, wealth,
and fancy clothes than about kindness, insight, and hard work.
Kansas City made him urban and urbane. Sammy says to him,
"You can never, now, get away from the world into which you

have gone" (p. 207). The narrative suggests that urban superficiality is alluring and captivating, but that persons of breeding can escape from it with great effort.

The immoral influence of the city is spreading as the world becomes less rural. At the end of the novel, Howitt meets a young artist from Chicago who has gone to the Ozarks for a summer, as his own son had done years before. Speaking to the young man about the mountains, Howitt says,

They will give you great treasure, that you may give again to others, who have not your good strength to escape from the things that men make and do in the restless world over there. One of your noble craft could scarcely fail to find the good things God has written on this page of His great book. Your brothers need the truths that you will read here, unless the world has greatly changed (pp. 296-97).

Howitt then says that the railroad will taint the mountains with city ways. "Many will come," he says, "and the beautiful hills that have been my strength and peace will become the haunt of careless idlers and a place of revelry" (p. 297). The imminence of the city's encroachment is pointed out by the artist the following summer. He sees a mountain near Howitt's grave being gouged for the railroad. The materialism of the city may be overcome at great cost, but the spread of the city is inevitable.

The Shepherd of the Hills suggests that an individual's spirituality, drawn from nature, is sufficient to overcome urban superficiality and to defeat those who have evil in their veins. The hero is Howitt, a city minister who seeks and finds a spiritual rebirth in the Ozarks. He teaches others to shun materialism and to gain self-mastery. Those who learn from him help defeat Wash Gibbs, who is shot to death trying to escape with stolen gold and whose body is torn apart by buzzards.

Howitt understands the restorative power of nature from the moment he arrives in the Ozarks. "I am not looking for mines of lead or zinc," he tells a curious native. "There is greater wealth in these hills and forests" (p. 8). The size of the mountains reflects the size of God, and their majesty can inspire peace and strength in an individual. Jesus recognized the spirituality of nature, as Howitt learns:

I never understood until the past months why the Master so often withdrew into the wilderness. There is not only food and medicine for one's body; there is also healing for the heart and strength for the soul in nature. One gets very close to God...in these temples of God's own building (p. 258).

Indeed, the restorative nature of the mountains is the result of God's creation; cities, conversely, are oppressive because they are human rather than divine creations:

We who live in the cities see but a little farther than across the street. We spend our days looking at the work of our own and our neighbors' hands. Small wonder our lives have so little of God in them, when we come in touch with so little that God has made (p. 19).

Spiritual depth comes with meditation on nature in the wilderness.

Inwardly restored and looking ten years younger, Howitt successfully spreads the gospel of God's nature to all of the inhabitants of Mutton Hollow. Grant Matthews says to him, "Don't you suppose we can see, sir, how you've made over the whole neighborhood? There ain't a family for ten miles that don't come to you when they're in trouble" (p. 144). Grant and his son learn to control the beast within, and Sammy Lane becomes wise and sophisticated while remaining warm and down to earth. Howitt becomes God's emissary. "What these hills have been to you," Grant Matthews tells him, "you have been to me" (p. 282). Deliverance from evil begins with the inspiration of nature, and is carried through by an enlightened individual.

Dad Howitt's spiritual renewal has definite purpose. From the majesty and calm of the Ozark Mountains he receives inner understanding to complement his outward faith, but he does not keep his heartfelt faith to himself. The mountains are a refuge, not a cloister. Howitt imparts his faith to mountaineers so that they too can experience the meaningfulness that their natural surroundings offer. Experienced and understood, nature overcomes the temptations of outwardness and materialism by instilling a sense of grand purpose. Nature, in other words, is God's chalkboard; one need only decipher the message in order to learn how to live.

After becoming enlightened himself, Howitt's first pupil is Sammy Lane, who not only makes a wise choice of a mate, but also gains a perspective that permits her to make wise choices. Howitt does not manipulate her choice, nor does she decide fortuitously.

Rather, he helps her discover the logic of nature on her own, as she exclaims,

Oh, Dad, I see it all, now; all that you have been trying in a thousand ways to teach me. You have led me into a new world, the real world, the world that has always been and must always be, and in that world man is king; king because he is a man. And the treasure of his kingdom is the wealth of his manhood (p. 209).

Sammy learns that it is nature's way, God's way, to value man over material, so she breaks her engagement to Ollie, telling him,

I know a little of life. And I have learned some things that I fear you have not. Besides, I know now that I do not love you. I have been slow to find the truth, but I have found it. And this is the one thing that matters, that I found it in time (pp. 207-208).

Sammy now understands the created order, and thus has a principle by which to live. Sammy overcomes her attraction to urban sophistication by learning "that the only common ground whereon men and women may meet in safety is the ground of their manhood and womanhood" (p. 290).

Howitt also leads the Matthews men to an understanding of the created order of nature. Whereas Sammy learned to value man over material, the Matthews learn to behave as men rather than beasts. Referring to Young Matt, Grant Matthews tells Howitt, "I know right well what he'd been if it wasn't for you to show him what the best kind of man's like" (p. 145). About himself Grant Matthews says, "Stayin' as you have after our talk that first night you come, an' livin' down here on this spot alone...it's just like I was a little kid, an' you was a standin' big and strong like between me an' a great blackness that was somethin' awful" (p. 145). With Howitt's tutelage, the Matthews men learn that God created humans to act on thought rather than impulse. Resolution in *The Shepherd of the Hills* follows the understanding of the order of God's creation. God's will is writ large in the mountains, as the narrative's references to Genesis attest. According to Preachin' Bill,

When God looked upon th' work of his hands an' called hit good, he war sure a-lookin' at this here Ozark country... 'Taint no wonder 't all, God rested when he made these here hills; he jes naturally had t' quit, fer he done his beatenest an' war plumb gin out (pp. 1-2).

Young Matt and Sammy Lane resemble Adam and Eve:

Two splendid creatures they were—masterpieces of the Creator's handiwork; made by Him who created man, male and female, and bade them have dominion "over every living thing that moveth upon the earth"; kings by divine right (p. 292).

The pattern for morality is embedded in nature, there to be discerned by those who look earnestly.

The Shepherd of the Hills never says exactly how to discern the moral laws embedded in nature. This novel is not nearly as formulaic as its near contemporary, *In His Steps*. Nevertheless, certain features of the way to achieve resolution are clear. Human beings must be receptive to the initiative that God took in the act of creation. Evidently, only those of "good stock" can participate in this moral quest. Those of good stock are persons whose parents are moral and whose very interest in the quest indicates their choice breeding. Moreover, the definition of morality as deciding to be what we are created to be is highly ambiguous, given that God's created order is discerned with only a wisp of corroboration such as biblical teaching.

Receptiveness to God's will imbedded in nature occurs in the wilderness. Howitt's faith was superficial until he left Chicago permanently for the mountains, and nowhere does the narrative suggest that true faith can exist in urban centers. Indeed, the narrative suggests the opposite: that faith is difficult if not impossible to experience in the city because inspiration comes from what God has created, and not through human inventions. Nature is a necessary but insufficient element in moral salvation—Sammy and the Matthews find enlightenment, but Wash Gibbs does not—but the city is an impediment to faith.

The only other characteristic of the quest to act according to the created order is determination. Those who become faithful and moral do not wait for inspiration. Faith comes through purposeful struggling. Howitt has to leave Chicago where he is wealthy and renowned and meditate in the mountains. Sammy has to study the best of western thought under the tutelage of Howitt, and Young Matt must do the same under Sammy's tutelage:

All through summer and fall, when the day's work was done, or on a Sunday afternoon, they were together, and gradually the woods and the hills, with all the wild life that is in them, began to have for the young man a new meaning; or, rather, he learned little by little to read the message that lay on the open pages. First a word here and there, then sentences, then paragraphs, and soon he was reading alone, as he tramped the hills for stray stock, or worked in the mountain field. The idle days of winter and the long evenings were spent in reading aloud from the books that had come to mean most to her (p. 290).

Guided thought prepares the mind to perceive the laws of nature.

Achieving resolution in *The Shepherd of the Hills* is a combination of grace and works. Grace is found in nature, both in the creation of the mountains and in the lineage of good blood. Grace is enacted, however, only with the devotion of great mental energy to becoming morally perceptive and the will to resist the tinsel charms of the city. Of course, the will and devotion are gifts to those with good blood. Understanding and morality come to those whom God has chosen.

At the end of the novel, Sammy and Young Matt have been married and Dad Howitt is growing old. He prophesies the encroachment of the city to a visiting artist:

Before many years a railroad will find its way yonder. Then many will come, and the beautiful hills that have been my strength and peace will become the haunt of careless idlers and a place of revelry. I am glad that I shall not be here (p. 297).

This disquiet is a postscript to an otherwise happy ending to a novel that posits the country as a place of health and religion, and the city as a place of corruption and hypocrisy. With the mechanization of the city comes religious mechanization, orthodoxy, which threatens to replace the peace of mind that comes from working with nature. In *The Shepherd of the Hills*, Wright—and his readers—envision a frontier of virgin nature and virtue, and they fear that it will pass.

The popularity of *The Shepherd of the Hills* is evident from the enormous sales figures as well as from the tourist industry which grew around Branson, Missouri after the publication of the novel (Milstead 1931). The Shepherd of the Hills Farm, formerly the homestead of the J.K. Ross family who became the Matthews family in the novel, is still a major tourist attraction in the area, and

Branson itself has become a large resort area where *The Shepherd of the Hills* is still performed as a stage play (Hendrickson 1925; Spurlock 1936; Baxter 1970).

Wright had decided to become a full-time writer if *The Shepherd of the Hills* was successful. Shortly after submitting the manuscript to the Book Supply Company, he left Lebanon, Missouri to preach at the Redlands, California Christian Church. He stayed in Redlands less than a year. *The Shepherd of the Hills* was a bestseller, so in 1908 he left the ministry, moved south to a ranch near Holtville, California in the Imperial Valley, and wrote a bestselling sequel, *The Calling of Dan Matthews*.

The Calling of Dan Matthews

Whereas *The Shepherd of the Hills* ended by doubting the likelihood that true religion—i.e., rural living—would survive the steady encroachment of the city, *The Calling of Dan Matthews* alleviates this doubt by suggesting that good individuals have the strength to resist corruption and that they can control urban industries so that they will benefit the public.

As the setting of *The Shepherd of the Hills* is central to that novel, so is the setting central to its sequel. Unlike its predecessor, however, *The Calling of Dan Matthews* is set in a city, Corinth. Corinth is a relatively new city, built beside railroad tracks a mile away from what became Old Corinth in hopes of becoming a center of travel and commerce. But the hopes were never realized, and the railroad passed through Corinth destined for greater cities, stopping only for water from Corinth's supply. Old Corinth, known for its academy and one of the academy's graduates, an insightful statesman, was abandoned by all but the poor, thus becoming a detached and forgotten slum. The only remnant of its namesake in Corinth was a cast-iron statue of the statesman which stood in the center of the town.

The statue symbolizes Corinth. Whereas the statesman had been vibrant, the statue made a prophet from a past era into a shrine, permanent and lifeless. The statue, like the character of the city, is cast-iron, hollow. It symbolizes forgotten hopes and contributes nothing to the present. It symbolizes most clearly the religious character of the city, which is long on churches and doctrines but short on Christian charity. According to Dr. Oldham, the statesman's friend who understands Corinth well,

How can an institution, or a system of theological beliefs—with cast-iron prejudices, cast-iron fidelity to issues long past and forgotten, cast-iron unconcern of vital issues of the life of today and cast-iron want of sympathy with the living who toil and fight and die on every side—how can such speak the great loving, sympathetic, helpful spirit of Him whose name only it bears, as that bears only the name of my friend? (p. 342)

This is the setting into which Dan Matthews, son of Young Matt and Sammy Lane from *The Shepherd of the Hills*, assumes the duties of his first pastorate. He is the new minister of Strong Memorial Church, which is controlled by two elders. One is Judge Strong, who is by far the largest financial contributor, but who is also an unscrupulous collector of real estate. The other is Nathaniel Jordan, as elderly dogmatist who cares much more about the church's good name than about the practice of Christian faith. From the outset, it is clear that Dan, who is naive and sincere, cannot survive in a church dominated by corruption and narrow-mindedness.

Dan's first faux pas is to rescue a handicapped boy from the town bully. Fresh off the train to Corinth, Dan witnesses a drunk man strike Denny Mulhall, leaving the helpless boy crumpled in the dirt. Instinctively, Dan protects the boy by beating the bully senseless, not understanding that this behavior was unfitting for a minister. Dan compounds his misjudgment by befriending the boy and his widowed mother, poor Irish Catholics who rarely attended church, much less a doctrinally sound church. Eyebrows in Corinth are raised because Dan does not act the way a minister is expected to.

Suspicions in Dan's church grow as his friendship with a pretty young nurse named Hope Farwell becomes common knowledge. Their relationship is chaste, but rumors spread partly because Elder Jordon's daughter wants to marry a young minister, and Hope thwarts her chances, and partly because Hope avoids church out of principle. She is a Christian with a well-worn, often-read Bible, but her discipleship leads her to serve her patients with deep-seated dedication and to reject institutional Christianity. The attraction between Hope and Dan is evident—they spend their free time together—so rumors about sexual liaisons begin to circulate.

These rumors are fueled when Hope befriends Charity Conner. Years before, Charity's father killed Jack Mulhall, the town marshall. The members of Strong Memorial Church, where Charity had taught Sunday school, responded by shunning her and by accusing her of promiscuity. As time passes, she can find no work, so instead of confirming the rumors by becoming a prostitute, she ingests carbolic acid in a suicide attempt. She is rescued, however, and Hope nurses her back to physical and emotional health. Hope and Charity move into a room at the house owned by Deborah Mulhall, the widow of the man Charity's father had murdered. The members of Strong Memorial Church ignore this act of forgiveness and understanding, focusing instead on the house of outcasts dear to Dan.

At this point, Dan's tenure as minister of Strong Memorial Church begins to wane. Not only is he friendly with people unpopular with those who control the church, but he preaches too much about Christian actions and too little about Christian dogmas. He is not satisfying the unwritten terms of his employment. The process of Dan's dismissal begins when he learns that Judge Strong is about to evict the Mulhalls for late payment of interest due on the house. (Deborah Mulhall cannot find work because she is a friend of Grace Conner.) Dan coerces Judge Strong to write a note that gives the widow a full year to pay the installment. Strong writes the note, but he begins the process of Dan's dismissal soon thereafter.

Shortly before Dan is fired, Deborah Mulhall's brother arrives in Corinth and tells them that he had paid the mortgage in gold years before. Dan gathers collaborative evidence from the bank; then he threatens to expose Strong unless he refunds all of the money that Deborah had paid to him. This Judge Strong does by sending the money with Elder Jordan, who pays Dan a visit. Jordan hands the money over and tells Dan not just that he is fired, but also that the church will not provide him with a letter of recommendation. Jordan prefers to forgive the thief who contributes handsomely to the church over exposing him and assuring that the church gets a bad reputation.

Dan leaves Corinth, but not before meeting up with the triumphant Judge Strong and demanding that he apologize for the aspersions he has cast upon Dan's friends. When Strong refuses, Dan beats him up.

Satisfied with this retribution, Dan returns to Mutton Hollow to supervise mining on his family's property. There he also meets up with Hope Farwell, who has been hired nearby as a nurse after Grace has enrolled in a nursing school. The two reaffirm their love for one another and decide to marry. Freed from the confines of institutional religion, each carries out a full Christian ministry, Hope caring for the sick and Dan excising minerals for the benefit of society. Dan has learned the nature of true discipleship, as he explains in his last sermon to Strong Memorial Church:

God is as truly in the fields of grain, in the forests, in the mines, and in those laws of Nature by which men convert the product of field and forest and mine into the necessities of life. Therefore these are as truly holy as this institution. Therefore, again, the ministry of farm, and mine, and factory, and shop; of mill, and railroad, and store, and office, and wherever men toil with strength of body or strength of mind for that which makes for the best life of their kind—that ministry is sacred and holy (p. 346).

The evil that *The Calling of Dan Matthews* addresses is within the church. The church is where the basest motives belie the highest ideals, where appearance counts for more than reality, where hypocrisy is the rule of the day. The Christianity of the churches is unchristian, as Harry Abbott, a doctor who often heals the indigent, tells Dan:

We see the church's lack of appreciation of true worth of character, we know the vulgar, petty scheming and wire-pulling for place, the senseless craving for notoriety, and the prostitution of the spirit of Christ's teaching to denominational ends. We understand how the ministers are at the mercy of the lowest minds and the meanest spirits in the congregation (p. 210).

In this novel, the only evil outside the church—the bully Jud Hardy taunting and striking the defenseless, handicapped Mulhall boy Denny—is quickly subdued; the evil in the church, which is much more powerful because it is insidious, endures without sign of abatement.

The hypocrisy of Strong Memorial Church, so named because of the power of wholesale commitment to an idealized past, is symbolized by two controlling elders, Judge Strong and Nathaniel Jordan. Strong maintains the appearance of piety by attending all church meetings and contributing heartily to the church coffers. Reliance on his support keeps him powerful and blinds people to his financial greed. After Dan forces him to extend the loan repayment schedule for the widow Mulhall, Judge Strong deftly orchestrates Dan's dismissal. First he fans rumors concerning Dan's morality; then he encourages others to question Dan's orthodoxy. As Dan's beliefs and behaviors come under increasing suspicion, Strong has a professional evangelist hired whose hypocrisy of greed and creed matches Strong Memorial's:

This evangelist...is that type of professional soul-winner evolved by the system whereby the church pays for the increase of its flock at so much per head, inasmuch as the number of his calls, and the amount of his hire depend upon the number of additions per meeting to the evangelist's credit. A soul-winner with small meetings to his credit receives a very modest compensation for his services, and short notices in the church papers. But the big fellows—those who have hundreds of souls per meeting, come higher, much higher; also they have more space given them in the papers, which helps them to come higher still. Souls may have depreciated in value since Calvary, but one thing is sure, the price of soul-winners has gone away up since the days of Paul and his fellow ministers (p. 314).

In consultation with Strong's followers, the evangelist agrees that Dan is ill-suited for the ministry.

After Dan confronts Judge Strong with evidence of theft, Strong makes restitution through Elder Jordan, who also delivers Dan's notice of termination. Jordan prefers to ignore Judge Strong's crime because it would tarnish the church's image. No matter that an elder is corrupt—Judge Strong keeps the church financially solvent. Jordan's hypocrisy equals Strong's. The exchange between Jordan and Dan about silence concerning Strong's crime reveals the hypocritical nature of the institutional church:

"Judge Strong is one of our leading members—an Elder. He has been for years. It would ruin us—ruin us!"

"But," said Dan coolly, "he is a thief. You must know that he stole this money. Here—," he stretched forth his hand, holding the envelope, "here is the confession of guilt."

The Elder's voice trembled again. "Brother Matthews! Brother Matthews! I—I protest! Such language applied to an Elder is unchristian; you know the scripture?"

"Is it not true?" persisted Dan.

"Ahem! Brother Strong may have made a mistake, may—ah, have done wrong, but the church—the church; we must think of the good name of the cause! Coming so soon after the revival, too!"

"Am I to understand, then, that the church will keep this man in his place as an Elder; that you will protect him when you know his true character?"

At the question the other stared blankly. "Why—why how could we get along without him?" (pp. 329-30)

Here the narrative explains the nature of evil in the institutional church. The church desires reputation more than character, and it disguises and rationalizes its sins in order to enhance its image. The church stands in need of a thorough cleansing, but it prefers to polish its veneer instead.

Hypocrisy is the result of Christianity being fashioned into an institution. Christianity does not produce the evils of hypocrisy; rather, goodness is hindered by the churches, the sects, the denominations—the institutions, as made by humans rather than by God. As Hope Farwell tells Dan,

This selfish, wasteful, cruel, heartless thing that men have built up around their opinions, and whims, and ambitions, has so come between the people and the Christianity of the Christ, that they are beginning to question if, indeed, there is anywhere such a thing as the true church (p. 103).

She then says, "To the churches Christianity has become a question of fidelity to a church and creed and not to the spirit of Christ" (pp. 105-106). The church resembles a corporation more than a fellowship; institutional needs overshadow human needs.

The institutional character of the church, and not most of the members, is responsible for its maleficence. As Dr. Oldham explains, the church misleads good-hearted individuals:

The best people in the world are sometimes held by evil circumstances which their own best intentions have created. The people in the church are the salt of the earth. If it were not for their goodness the system would have rotted long ago. The church, for all its talk, doesn't save the people; the people save the church (p. 336).

As people learn to believe that religious institutions are divine rather than human creations, they become servants of those institutions rather than of God.

The church qua institution is at fault. As faith becomes more corporate and less individual, it is supplanted by institutional imperatives. One of these imperatives is the need for financial security. The corrupt Judge Strong is powerful in the local church and in the denomination because he keeps them financially stable: "A heavy contributor to the general work and missionary funds to which the leaders looked for the practical solutions to their modest bread and butter problems, he had the ears of them all" (pp. 298-99).

Another institutional imperative is that its members toe the party line. Dan is acceptable in the beginning when he preaches doctrinal sermons like "The Faith of the Fathers" (pp. 78-79), but he incurs objections when he begins to preach on truly spiritual themes like "Fellowship of Service" (p. 227). In addition to financial and intellectual imperatives, the institutional church requires a favorable public image. Elder Jordan warns Dan to stay away from Grace Connor and Hope Farwell: "We do not think that you mean any harm, but your standing in the community, you know, is such that we must shun every appearance of evil" (p. 199).

The institutional church is not merely in the business of money, or belief, or appearance; it is equally in the business of personal power. As Strong Memorial Church was controlled by two elders, one immoral and the other misguided, so the denomination was controlled by political maneuvering that bore no relation to spirituality:

There were the leaders, regularly appointed by the denomination, who were determined to keep that which had been committed to them, at any cost; and to this end glorified, in the Lord's service, the common, political methods of distributing the places of conspicuous honor and power, upon program and committee, among those friends and favorites who could be depended upon to respond most emphatically, or who were—in the vernacular—"safe." Equally active, with methods as familiar but not equally in evidence—for one must be careful—were the would-be leaders, who—"for the glory of Christ"—sought these same seats of the mighty, and who were assisted by those who aspired to become their friends and favorites—joint heirs in their success should they succeed (p. 297).

The church is Christian in name only. Controlled by status seekers who support the institutional ethos, the church is hypocritical and cannot help but cause the evils of hypocrisy with which true Christianity must do battle.

The church is evil because it is a human institution; therefore, the antidote to the problems it fosters does not lie in the creation of yet another church. An alternative church would still be an institution and therefore corrupt. Dr. Oldham explains this principle to Dan: "Every reformation begins with the persecution of the reformer and ends with the followers of that reformer persecuting those who would lead them another step toward freedom" (p. 337). Dan takes the doctor's observation to heart. After he preaches his final sermon in Strong Memorial Church, a farmer friend of his named John Gardner suggests that a group from the church form another with Dan as their pastor. But Dan responds, "I have thought of the possibility you mention, but I can't do it. You do not need another church in Corinth. You have more than you need now" (p. 344).

Rather than forming another church, the solution to the evils of the institutional church lies in individuals working in the spirit of service to others. When Dan turns the farmer's offer down, the farmer says, "I suppose I'll keep right on being a church member, but I reckon I'll have to find most of my religion in my work." Dan tells him, "If you cannot find God in your everyday work, John, you'll not find Him on Sunday at the church" (p. 344).

As the farmer finds salvation in his work, so do Dan and his friends. Dan returns to Mutton Hollow to supervise the Matthews' mines. "God put the wealth in the mountains, not for us alone, but for all men," his father tells him. "So it has been to us a sacred trust, which we have never felt that we were fitted to administer. We have always hoped that our first born would accept it as his life work—his ministry" (p. 360).

Dan marries Hope, who continues her ministry of nursing. She is a dedicated Christian and Bible-reader who refuses to attend church. "Man serves God only by serving men," she says. "There can be no ministry but the ministry of man to man" (p. 105). Grace enrolls in nursing school to "fit herself for her chosen ministry" (p. 309). Christian service, the antidote to the institutional church's evils, lies outside the church. *The Calling of Dan Matthews* suggests that abandoning the church can enhance true Christian ministries.

Resolving the evils of hypocrisy requires ministry, or vocation. However, ministry is not necessarily professional in the sense of church or denominational ordination. By contrast, it is personal, individual, the integration of work with one's physical, intellectual, and emotional characteristics. The idea of ministry in *The Calling of Dan Matthews* extends the idea of nature in *The Shepherd of the Hills* beyond a general sense that God instituted morality along the same principles by which God created nature to the individual's choice of vocation.

The choice of Christian vocation is Dan's major struggle. Dan is pure, both in body and in mind, and he decides to become a professional minister because he believes it to be the noblest vocation. He had, according to the narrative, "unusual beauty and strength of body, and uncommon fineness of mind" (p. 28), making him "a revelation of...that best part of the race" (p. 32). His choice of the ministry was logical, given these characteristics and his upbringing:

the first born of this true mating of a man and woman who had never been touched by those forces in our civilization which so dwarf and cripple the race, but who had been taught in their natural environment those things that alone have the power to truly refine and glorify life (p. 32).

In his first conversation with Hope Farwell, Dan explains his choice of vocation simply: "the ministry is, to me, the highest service to which a man may be called" (p. 104).

Hope tries to expand his definition of ministry in that conversation, telling him, "Man serves God only by serving men. There can be no ministry but the ministry of man to man" (p. 105). Dan also learns that ministers are hampered both by their title and by their employers. Hope prophesies Dan's experience when she tells him that a minister

is a man set apart from all those who live lives of service, who do the work of the world. And then that he should be distinguished from these world-workers, these servers, by this noblest of all titles—a minister, is the bitterest irony that the mind of the race ever conceived (p. 105).

As a minister, Dan is not perceived as a man but as a " 'Reverend,' 'Brother,' the preacher" (p. 57). He finds such labeling so oppressive and limiting that he escapes to farm work, gardening, and fishing as often as he can. However, Dan decides to change vocations, not merely from listening to the arguments that Hope makes or from bridling at the labels, but because he experiences and learns to understand the disparity between his principles and the realities of the professional ministry:

It was because Dan had believed so strongly, so wholly in the ministry of the church that he had failed. Had he not accepted so unreservedly, and given himself so completely to the ministry as it was presented to him in theory, had he in some degree doubted, he would have been able to adjust himself to the actual conditions. He would have succeeded (p. 339).

Dan leaves the ministry to serve humanity by supervising lead and zinc mines and to marry the woman of his choice, Hope Farwell, whose Christian ministry of nursing is as passionate as her avoidance of the church.

Although the narrative suggests that Christian vocations are usually found outside the institutional church, it does leave room, however small, for ministry within the church. This minor equivocation concerns the character of Denny Mulhall, the young man whose childhood accident left him partially paralyzed and whose poverty forced him to abandon his dream of studying for the priesthood. Before Dan forces Judge Strong to repay the money he stole from Denny's mother, Denny is described as "forever barred from the life his whole soul craved, yearning for books and study with all his heart, but forced to give the last atom of his poor strength in digging in the soil for the bare necessities of life, denied even a pittance to spend for the volumes he loved" (p. 270). However, after Judge Strong provides restitution, Denny's church vocation is realized:

Denny...has received his education and—surrounded now by the books he craved—cultivates another garden, wherein he bids fair to grow food for men quite as necessary as cabbages or potatoes. Deborah is proud and happy with her boy; who, though he be crippled in body, has a heart and mind stronger than given to many (p. 356).

The fact that Denny's choice of the ministry is lauded while Dan's is not—both are endowed with great intelligence and compassion—may be explained by Denny's paralysis, which makes him ill-suited for the type of work that Dan's physical prowess suits him for. The difference may also lie in Dan's yearning for a mate, something that Denny never exhibits, probably because of his handicap. (This would also explain why it is "natural" for him to become a celibate priest and equally "natural" for Dan to marry.) These two choices, one for the ministry and one against, illustrate that the choice of Christian vocation, the object of moral behavior in this novel, is based on the application of one's mental and physical characteristics to the idea of service to one's fellows. The morality values a high degree of individuality and assumes that the world operates on knowable divine principles.

The novel does not explicitly tell how to find one's true Christian vocation. The decision is neither mysterious—admonitions do not come through dreams or visions or even vague feelings—nor is it mechanical—no character explains the steps to achieve resolution. Instead, those who choose wisely do so because they are virtuous from the start. The virtuous either choose right early in life, or they are led by their experiences and their opportunities to choose the fitting Christian service.

Most of the protagonists choose Christian ministries with little consternation. The health professions are prima facie right choices, because Hope Farwell and Grace Connor decide effortlessly to become nurses, and John Oldham and Harry Abbott choose easily to be physicians. Likewise, Denny Mulhall's desire to become a priest is delayed only by the means to becoming one; the decision is never doubted. Apparently, the choices made by good people will almost always be right.

Only Dan makes an error. He became a minister out of good intention, but with matching naiveté. Once he understands the hypocrisy of the institutional church, he knows that he must choose another avenue of Christian service. Having been introduced to the head of a mining company by Dr. Oldham, being in a family that owns land rich in minerals, and being an individual well-suited for physical work, Dan chooses the right alternative for him: supervising mining operations.

Thus the method for deciding one's Christian vocation requires good intentions and opportunity. Both are providential. There is no conversion here; the good overcome the effects of hypocrisy, while the hypocritical are left behind. Nature takes care of those who understand nature; those who rely upon human institutions reap what petty rewards institutions have to offer.

The Book Supply Company set aside $48 thousand for full-page announcements of *The Calling of Dan Matthews* and its two predecessors in newspapers and magazines. An advertisement in *Publishers' Weekly* stated: " 'I have done my best—another chapter in my ministry to the race—Author,' " Wright's books were also for the first time made available to regular booksellers through the distributors Reilly & Lee. The success was swift: The first printing of *The Calling of Dan Matthews,* some 100 thousand copies, sold out within eight months (Mott 1947, 299).

The Wright Man

In Imperial Valley, California, Wright wrote three of his five bestsellers: *The Calling of Dan Matthews* (1909), *The Winning of Barbara Worth* (1911), and *The Eyes of the World* (1914). He wrote these novels at Tecolote Rancho, "Owl Ranch," in an 18 x 35-foot ramada that he built with thatched arrow-weed. In 1910, Reynolds moved to a ranch home near Pamona, California, turning over the management of the Book Supply Company to his son, Elsbery Washington Reynolds, III.

During this period, Wright was in his prime as a bestselling novelist. He had sold some two million copies of his two religious novels, and he wrote three more bestsellers, sermon texts still, but no longer ostensibly religious. The first of these was *The Winning of Barbara Worth,* a story which pitted a benevolent western capitalist against a self-serving eastern plutocrat. Whereas the former "sought to make Capital serve the race," the other "served Capital" (p. 395). Capitalism, according to the novel, is a neutral economic system, made good or bad by the individuals in control:

The methods of The King's Basin Land and Irrigation Company in La Palma de la Mano de Dios were the methods of capital impersonal, inhuman—the methods of a force governed by laws as fixed as the laws of nature, neither cruel nor kind; inconsiderate of man's misery or happiness, his life or death; using man for its own ends—profit, as men use water and soil and sun and air. The methods of Jefferson Worth were the methods of a man laboring with his brother men, sharing their hardships, sharing their returns; a man using money as a workman uses his tools to fashion and build and develop, adding thus to the welfare of human kind. It was inevitable that the Company and Jefferson Worth should war (p. 395).

The benevolent western capitalist wins over his malevolent eastern foe. *The Winning of Barbara Worth* proclaimed that community and prosperity can be accomplished by those who reject eastern, urban practices and use capital to serve the public good.

The Winning of Barbara Worth was promoted even more rigorously that its two bestselling predecessors. The Book Supply Company allocated more than $75 thousand to advertising, mostly in the form of full-page advertisements for the latest Harold Bell Wright novel as well as insets reminding readers about the other ones. Other sales techniques included inserting a postcard in each copy of a book, which the reader could send to a friend, recommending it or another Wright novel as "one of the best I have ever read." The postcard contained useful quotations from the novel, and booksellers were provided with stacks of them, so that a collector could obtain the entire series. Wright also gladly sold the rights to his novels to playwrights, whose tent-show adaptations played to millions of people who were likely to buy the book after having seen the play (Nye 1970, 40).

The promotion was effective. The first printing of *The Winning of Barbara Worth*, 175 thousand copies, sold out within one month (Mott 1947, 230). Eventually more than 900 thousand copies were sold.

Undoubtedly the extensive promotion of Wright's novels helped to put them on the public agenda, but their phenomenal successes cannot be attributed to advertising alone, at least not beyond the first printing or two. The less rigorous promotion of Wright's earlier books, which became bestsellers, suggests that Wright's popularity had at least as much to do with positive word-of-mouth reports as it did with advertising campaigns. By the time that *The Winning of Barbara Worth* was published, Wright has already won a following, so that the advertisements served more as notices that another Wright novel was available than as inducements to buy an unknown product. The campaigns were efforts to maximize, not create, sales of books by an already popular author. Clearly readers found Wright's didacticism agreeable.

A prophet may not be accepted in his hometown, but Wright won Imperial Valley almost immediately. In 1915, the Hotel Barbara Worth began business in El Centro (the hotel burned down in 1962) and a country club near Holtville was named the Barbara Worth Country Club. There is a Barbara Worth Junior High School in Brawley and a Barbara Worth Road which runs north and south just past the west side of Tecolote Rancho (Harris).

Three years after the publication of *The Winning of Barbara Worth*, the Book Supply Company brought out the next Wright bestseller, *The Eyes of the World* (1914), a fictional diatribe against art critics and high art, which the novel holds to be dishonest and prurient perpetrators of a corrupt society. The main character, Aaron King, nearly succumbs to the temptations of fame, money, and social position which would be his if he pleased the urban, monied patrons of the arts. A novelist, famous as a result of having sacrificed his integrity for wealth and popularity, warns King:

"To acquire fame, you have only to paint pictures of fast women who have no morals at all—making them appear as innocent maidens, because they have the price to pay, and, in the eyes of the world, are of social importance. Put upon your canvases what the world will call portraits of distinguished citizens— making low-browed money-thugs to look like noble patriots, and bloody butchers of humanity like benevolent saints. You need give yourself no uneasiness about your success. It is easy. Get in with the right people; use your family name and your distinguished ancestors; pull a few judicious advertising wires; do a few artistic stunts; get yourself into the papers long and often, no matter how; make yourself a fad; become a pet of the social autocrats—and your fame is assured. And—you will be what I am" (pp. 44-45).

However, King resists the temptation, changing the portrait of a seductive and wealthy patron which he had begun as a painting of an innocent virgin into a painting of "the hideous vulgarity, the intellectual poverty, and the moral depravity" (p. 315) that lay just beneath her poise and pseudo-beauty. He entitles this painting "The Spirit of the Age." He also paints "The Spirit of Nature," which reflects the virtues and beauty of a country girl, who he marries at the very end of the novel. Once King decides to do honest work, he loses his anguish and gains peace of mind which, in *The Eyes of the World* as well as Wright's other novels, is the result of personal integrity and the respect of unassuming rural people.

In an interview after the publication of *The Eyes of the World*, Wright revealed how he emphasized moral messages without pretense to literariness:

"When I start to write a novel, the first thing I do is figure out why I am going to write it. Not what is the story, but why? I mull this over a while, and when it is pretty straight in my mind, I write out an argument. No suggestion of plot, you see. No incidents, scenes, location, nothing done at first except the argument, but it is the heart and soul of the novel. The novel is merely this argument presented throughout the medium of characters, plot, incidents, and the other properties of the story. Next come the characters, each standing for some element or factor in the argument. Up to the last copying of *The Eyes of the World*, not a character had been named. They were called in the copy, Greed, Ambition, Youth, or whatever they represented to me in the writing of the story" (Overton 1923, 129-30).[3]

Wright's explanation that he wrote the *Eyes of the World* and his other novels as moral arguments overlaid with narrative devices underscores the strong didactic character of his novels. Indeed, whether ostensibly religious or not, Wright's novels were fictional sermons with an allegorical character similar to John Bunyan's *Pilgrim's Progress.* The complexity of the melodrama may have attracted readers, but the stories' morals are so pronounced that readers would have found the messages tolerable if not agreeable, given that they bought Wright's novels in mammoth quantities. Wright's bestsellers were sermons that found an eager national congregation. With the encouragement of $100 thousand advertising budget for *The Eyes of the World,* some 750 thousand copies sold in little over a month. Eventually, 925 thousand copies were sold (Mott 1947, 231).

After he published *The Eyes of the World,* Wright left California for Arizona, where he set up a camp in which to write *When a Man's a Man,* his last bestseller. There in 1916, while on horseback, Wright was struck by a car, which broke his ribs. He contracted tuberculosis again. However, he recovered as he put the novel together, writing mostly outdoors so that he could get as much sunshine as possible (Wright 1924; Millard 1917).

Wright published *When a Man's a Man* on schedule in 1916. Again the Book Supply Company spent $100 thousand to promote the novel, and 600 thousand copies were sold in advance (Mott 1947, 231). This novel is nothing less than a hymn to virility. Manhood, which can be obtained through honest, physical work, is identified with the west and is characterized by strength, courage, sincerity, honesty, and usefulness, the same virtues that apply to Wright's protagonists in his other novels. Effeminacy, identified with easterners and city slickers, is connected to culture, cleverness, manners, success, and social position. This argument if most direct in *When a Man's a Man,* but it is very much present in Wright's novels all the way back to *That Printer of Udell's*; indeed, in his religious novels, wheat refers to "real men," muscular, honest, hardworking country men, and chaff refers to dogmatic or wealthy pretenders, cultured, clever, upper crust, polished city dwellers. In *The Shepherd of the Hills,* Dad Howitt has to leave Chicago to tend sheep, and in *When a Man's a Man,* Lawrence Knight has to leave Cleveland to punch steers. Devotion to God and virility are complementary qualities of persons who choose rural life over city life. The sacredness of virile life in the wilderness is clear from the very beginning of *When a Man's a Man*:

> There is a land where a man, to live, must be a man.
> It is a land of granite and marble and porphyry and gold—and a man's strength must be as the strength of the primeval hills. It is a land of oaks and cedars and pines—and a man's mental grace must be as the grace of the untamed trees. It is a land of far-arched and unstained skies, where the wind sweeps free and untainted, and the atmosphere is the atmosphere of those places that remain as God made them—and a man's soul must be as the unstained skies, the unburdened wind, and the untainted atmosphere (p. 11).

The city-country dichotomy is only one division that runs throughout Wright's bestsellers. There is, as van Benschoten illustrates, a strong class-consciousness and racial and ethnic prejudice (1968, 379). In *The Calling of Dan Matthews*, Grace Connor is forced to live in a black neighborhood because she is shunned by the town's whites, and she tries to commit suicide. Dr. Abbott, who has saved her just in time, says to Hope, a nurse, "She tried so hard to die, nurse; she will try again the moment she regains consciousness. These good colored people would do anything for her, but she must see one of her own race when she opens her eyes" (p. 151). Later, another doctor explains Grace's suicide attempt:

> "She wanted to live, to be strong and beautiful like you. But this community with its Churches and Sunday schools and prayer meetings wouldn't let her. They denied her the poor privilege of working for the food she needed. They refused even a word of real sympathy. They hounded her into this stinking hole to live with the negroes" (p. 156).

In this bestseller, to live with blacks is a fate deserving death. Blacks may be good people, but the races must be kept separated.

Blacks are not the only group beneath whites in Wright's bestsellers. Indians and Chicanos are likewise inferior. In *The Winning of Barbara Worth*, the non-whites threaten violence because there has been a delay in available money to pay them:

> "We have promised these greasers and Indians that we will pay to-morrow without fail. When we don't pay, on top of all the trouble we have had, no explanation will stand. They'll go on the warpath sure. If they were white men it would be different" (p. 380).

The message is clear: Hardworking blue-collar and middle class whites are superior to the majority of rich whites and to all people of other racial and national origins.

Wright After Bestsellers

When a Man's a Man was Wright's last hurrah. He continued to publish, but his popularity had subsided. In 1920 he was divorced, and he was remarried to the former Mary Potter Duncan, and in 1921 he left the Book Supply Company for D. Appleton and Company (Overton 1925, 92). Elsbery Washington Reynolds, III moved to California in 1919, leaving the treasurer of the Book Supply Company, Louis N. Black, to run the company. The Reynolds family, busy growing citrus and selling Studebakers in Pamona, California, sold the Book Supply Company to Black in 1925. In 1927, Wright returned to the characters of *The Shepherd of the Hills* and *The Calling of Dan Matthews* in *God and the Groceryman*, but the trilogy idea failed. Wright's novels sold less and less. In 1932, Wright left Appleton for Harpers, explaining in a letter to J.W. Hiltman, president of Appleton, his reasons for doing so. "For reasons which in my estimation justify the decision, I shall not offer another book to D. Appleton & Company," Wright said.

> From the first year of my connection with you I have been disappointed and dissatisfied with the policies under which you have marketed my books. . . .
> From the beginning of our association I have checked your advertising with the advertising given other authors by other publishers. In this also you have placed my work at a disadvantage which I feel justifies my dissatisfaction (Wright 1931).

Appleton had promoted Wright's novels extensively—even circulating a ten-inch Victor Red Seal recording of Wright reading from *Helen of the Old House*—although not with the single-mindedness with which the Book Supply Company had marketed his bestsellers (Hawthorne 1923a, 1923b; Overton 1923; Tebbel 1987; Williams 1927).[4] In his reply to Wright's letter, Hiltman explained that Wright's declining popularity had little to do with marketing:

> When you came to us it was on a declining market for your work and we spent many thousands of dollars on every title that we published, to try and regain your market, in excess of a normal advertising expenditure; but not only ours but Burt's reprints also have been failing in sales (Hiltman 1931).

Wright's association with Harper and Brothers did not bolster the sales of his books. His first novel for Harpers, *Ma Cinderella* (1932), was not even able to recoup the advance against royalties. "MA CINDERELLA got off to a fine start, and that's about all we can say for it," wrote William H. Briggs, Wright's editor at Harpers (1933). Wright's response to this news surprised the staff at Harpers. "I have the humble suspicion that 'Ma Cinderella' did not sell enough to make good to Harpers the advance royalties which they paid me," Wright wrote to Briggs. "If my guess is right and 'Ma' fell short of the royalties advanced I want to know it right now so that I can send Harpers a check for the difference between what I have received from them and what 'Ma' earned up to Jan 1st" (1933a). Five weeks later, Wright sent a check to Harpers for $5,622.36 (Wright 1933b). The following summer, when he was preparing his autobiography, Wright wrote his editor, "THERE WILL BE NO ADVANCE ROYALTIES ON THIS BOOK NOR ANY BOOK OF MINE WHICH HARPERS MAY PUBLISH IN THE FUTURE UNTIL BUSINESS JUSTIFIES SUCH ADVANCES" (Wright 1933c). Wright appears to have been far more interested in the reception of his books than in the money they might make for him.

Wright was making money, but from a different source. He had turned to film, writing original screen plays and seeing his bestsellers made into movies: "The Winning of Barbara Worth" starring Gary Cooper (1926), "The Eyes of the World" (1930), "When a Man's a Man" (1938), "The Calling of Dan Matthews" (1936), and "The Shepherd of the Hills" starring John Wayne (1941).

In 1942, Harpers published Wright's last novel, *The Man who Went Away*. In typical Wright fashion, it concerned a businessman from New York who takes refuge in a pristine redwood forest which he owns, having lost his fortunes in the Great Depression. The businessman's original purpose was to sell the lumber, but after a spiritual regeneration, he donates the forest to the Save-the-Redwoods League. According to Mott, the novel was "stillborn" (1947, 232). Wright had long ago lost the audience eager for an anti-city social melodrama.

Harold Bell Wright died on 24 May 1944 of bronchial pneumonia in La Jolla, California. He is buried in San Diego beneath a large glass case which contains photographs and other keepsakes. All told, he wrote 21 novels and 15 movies.

In his autobiography, Wright gave this assessment to his work:

> I am not concerned as to whether or not my books will live after I am gone. If any book of mine shall live, it will be because it meets some vital need in human life. If, in the years to come, there should be no need for the truths I have endeavored to place before my fellows, then certainly my books shall and ought to be forgotten. If I have succeeded in touching the lives of those for whom I have written, in any degree, as my mother touched my life, I ask for no better immortality. As for that jade 'Fame,' the hussy is a sorry old flirt, and I have seen that those who dally with her reap infinitely more pain than pleasure. I simply am not interested (1934, 254).

Of course, Wright has not endured, but his bestsellers are highly significant nevertheless. Like other popular media, they are indicators of the social values of a large portion of the middle class. If Wright's frontier melodramas idealized a past, they reflected his readers' discomfort with the urbanization and industrialization and mechanization of the era. If Wright's religion was more manly work ethic than Christianity, Wright's readers were more interested in day-to-day practicality than in heady or emotional spirituality. Wright has not endured because he was too closely tied to his era; he can speak about the past to us, but he has nothing to say for our present. In this respect, Wright's novels are a quintessential revealer of pre-World War I American values, particularly religious ones.

Chapter Five

The Individual and the Middle Class

Students of American religion typically think of the dawning of the twentieth century as the time of the social gospel, when the writings of Ely, Gladden, and Rauschenbusch were influencing religious thought and perhaps even public policy. To an extent, this conception is correct. The social gospel intellectuals influenced their students in divinity schools, and they left a legacy in Christian social ethics—one need only read the books of Reinhold Niebuhr to see their lasting impression. They were also social reformers during the era of progressivism, and insofar as they supported the passage of anti-trust laws and the growth of federal regulatory agencies, they successfully fought the inevitable cruelties of unrestricted industrial capitalism. No doubt the social gospel thinkers were important for, and somehow symbolic of, the time.

Despite their importance, it is a mistake to identify them with the character of American religion at the turn of the century. By and large, Americans were not reading Ely, Gladden, or Rauschenbusch. The leaders of the social gospel movement were read by intellectuals; otherwise, their impact was mostly restricted to their locales—Ely at Johns Hopkins University and the University of Wisconsin, Gladden at First Congregational Church in Columbus, Ohio, and Rauschenbusch at Second German Baptist Church in New York and Rochester Theological Seminary. These writers may represent the direction of early twentieth-century theological ethics, but that says little about American religious values in general.

This period in American life is also known as the Third Great Awakening, which suggests a nationwide receptiveness to evangelical Protestantism. Whereas the social gospel was a liberal

98

middle-class perspective, the revivalism of Dwight Moody and Billy Sunday represented a conservative working-class perspective. "Revivalism" undoubtedly captures something of the spirit of American religion at the time, given the steadiness with which evangelists commanded capacity crowds, not to mention the tradition that they passed on to evangelists such as Billy Graham. But because revivals are by nature infrequent, ephemeral, and emotional affairs, they are unreliable indicators of American religious values in the same way that rock concerts are unreliable indicators of the American youth culture. Certainly the social gospel and evangelicalism are important features of American religion at the turn of the century, but they represent only part of the religious character of the era.

A fruitful way to ascertain common religious values is to examine the beliefs that underlie the most popular religious books of the era. (The same could [and should] be done, of course, for newspapers and magazines, but that would require a different analytical method because their content is much more diverse.) Because the mass media both reflect and shape cultural attitudes and values through a complex process of negotiation between audience and text, the bestselling religious novels during the early twentieth century are expressions of the central religious dialogues of the era. *In His Steps, Black Rock, The Shepherd of the Hills,* and *The Calling of Dan Matthews,* books which sold to one out of a hundred Americans, are records of the American religious character.

As the social gospel is an expression of liberal religious intellectuals and revivalism is an expression of evangelicals, the values in these novels typify the mainstream of the middle-class, those with the money and the desire to buy and read novels. The beliefs that underlie the most popular religious titles of the day therefore reveal only part of the American religious character. However, this part is a crucial counterbalance to the social gospel-revivalism dichotomy as an explanation of American religion in the early twentieth century.

The values within bestselling religious fiction become clear when examined according to the five elements of a culture's belief system: the nature of evil, the source of evil, the source of good, the nature of resolution, and the method of attaining resolution. Applied to the four religious bestsellers between 1897 and World

War I, they reveal that the middle class, troubled by urban life, believed with the social gospellers that Christianity had a large social responsibility, but that, with the evangelicals, this responsibility was best enacted voluntarily by beneficent individuals. Creeds mattered much less than deeds.

Nature of Evil

In each of the religious bestsellers of this period, evil involves the selfishness of individuals. The novels do not condemn whole classes or races or nations; instead, they condemn the selfish behavior of particular individuals. Selfishness is individuality gone awry; evil people are those whose desire for self-gratification injures others.

In *In His Steps*, selfishness takes two forms: self-satisfaction among the rich and sensuality among the poor. Because the affluent are content with the status quo, they ignore the plight of the unemployed, even when they are asked for help, refuse to outlaw liquor, even though it causes crime and death, perpetuate the squalor of the tenements for the sake of profits, and continue disreputable business practices regardless of the alienation and prurience they foster. Likewise, the poor are so content with their alcoholic debauchery that they fight local option and prefer whiskey to steady work. Very few of the poor will even take the initiative to beg, preferring instead the oblivion of drunkenness. Both the rich and the poor resist change because it requires sacrifice. Evil individuals will give up nothing for the benefit of others.

Selfishness in *Black Rock* has a quality of recklessness. The men work in the western mining camp in order to save enough money to be reunited with their wives and children, but on their quarterly payday they often succumb to the temptation to drink their loneliness away. While they are drunk, they gamble and fight. These periodic sprees cost lives and entire paychecks, always with the same result: the continued separation of families. Some men learn self-control, but most continue to seek immediate self-gratification even at the cost of remaining in the very predicament from which they crave escape.

The Shepherd of the Hills describes selfishness in terms of materialism. The most despicable character in the novel is a bully who will do anything to get what he wants, including robbery, assault, murder, and rape. He presents a danger for the heroine, who must learn to reject an equally selfish, but much gentler, man—

her fiancé. His method is status and money rather than muscle and gun, but he has the same degree of selfishness. In this bestseller, selfishness is double-edged: It harnesses the individual to a life of spiritual vacuousness as it causes physical and emotional pain or death for others.

In *The Calling of Dan Matthews*, selfishness runs rampant in the church. One of the elders is so controlled by his desire to collect real estate that he proceeds to steal property from a poor woman and her handicapped child. After the new minister forces him to relent, he instigates gossip and orchestrates the minister's dismissal. The other elder is so preoccupied with enhancing the church's image that he protects his malevolent associate and even delivers the notice of the minister's termination. The church is hypocritical because it is characterized by selfishness rather than by service.

Source of Evil

Individual selfishness is a sin of the heart, but its source is exterior. Although there are traces of biological determinism in *The Shepherd of the Hills*, the texts generally agree that evil is exacerbated if not caused by institutions. In one sense, these novels place the final blame for evil-doing on the choices that some individuals make; that is, strong individuals can survive institutional pressure. But corporate pressure is powerful, so that otherwise good individuals act selfishly because of their institutional environment.

The kindest treatment of institutions is in *In His Steps*. The church as an institution has failed the poor and the working class, alienating them from the source of moral strength and direction. Likewise, the legality of liquor and its availability in numerous saloons keep the poor unemployed and immoral, just as the tenements in which they live promote disease and premature death. But institutions are not bad by nature. Christians can change the church, pass Prohibition, and overhaul the slums. Diseased institutions infect the public; healthy institutions can heal the public. *In His Steps* blames the plight of the poor on bad institutions rather on institutions as such.

Black Rock exhibits a similar ambivalence towards institutions. The men in the mining camp are basically good at heart, but their periodic—and pathetic and dangerous—debaucheries are the result of the saloon being the only outlet for their frustration and loneliness. The proprietor is ultimately to blame for the saloon, but it is his saloon that promotes evil. But the saloon is not evil because it is an institution; the institution is evil because it is a saloon. Once Slavin changes his ways, he promotes good will in the camp by means of another institution: a recreation facility. In both *Black Rock* and *In His Steps,* evil is largely the fault of institutions run by selfish individuals and not the fault of institutions as such.

Harold Bell Wright thought differently. *The Shepherd of the Hills* blames the institutional character of cities for much of the world's evils. As human creations, cities hide the will of God, which is only apparent in virgin nature. Dad Howitt has to abandon Chicago for the Ozark Mountains in order to authenticate his faith, and once there, his mission is to dissuade Sammy from going to Kansas City and losing hers. Institutions are *ipso facto* bad in this narrative.

They fare no better in the sequel. *The Calling of Dan Matthews* condemns the church for being an institution which, by its nature, must be insular, self-serving, and often malicious. "Wherever two or three are gathered in His name, something suspicious is going on" is this novel's theme. The church is a place of political scheming, financial corruption, character assassination, and lying; good deeds take place outside the church. The hero and the heroine, dedicated Christians both, can minister to others' needs only on their own, away from the church. *In His Steps* and *Black Rock* hold out hope for the redemption of institutions; hope in the Wright novels rests only in their abandonment.

Source of Good

Although institutions are the greatest tempters, individuals are the greatest saviors. Heroes sometimes choose to create beneficent institutions to help the needy on a regular basis—this is particularly true of the two earliest bestsellers—but in all of the novels, it is an enlightened individual who leads people to repent of their unbridled selfishness.

The primary source of good in *In His Steps* is Reverend Maxwell. He is the one who teaches his congregation the meaning of Christian life, and he is their main resource as they seek to live by the vow always to do as Jesus would. Christian institutions, such as a Christian newspaper and a Christian settlement house, do result, but they are Christian because the individuals who control them have taken the vow. The newspaper follows the editorial and advertising policies that the editor determines, small businesses institute profit-sharing at the will of their owners, and settlement houses are created because certain disciples discern the need. The source of good in this novel is always an individual who may or may not decide to operate a Christian institution.

This principle also applies to *Black Rock*. The hero in this novel is also a minister whose role is to coordinate the good deeds at the mining camp. To keep the men from spending their pay on whiskey, Mr. Craig organizes a day of sports and entertainment, followed by a church service. After the service, he solicits volunteers to promise to abstain from drinking and to help their co-workers to do the same. Craig's hope for a coffee house to replace the saloon is realized when the barkeeper repents. Institutions may be socially beneficial, but only if good individuals manage them.

The Shepherd of the Hills takes a dimmer view of institutions, but it has strong faith in the power of individual regeneration. As Dad Howitt learns to discern the laws of nature in the mountains, his faith deepens. He imparts his wisdom to the mountaineers, who in turn learn to resist the temptations of materialism in themselves and to combat the materialism of their chief foe. The ultimate source of goodness is nature, but nature becomes effectual only when individuals receive enlightenment from it.

The most adamant expression of individuals being the source of good is in *The Calling of Dan Matthews*. In this novel, goodness can come only from individuals because institutions are necessarily corrupt. Dan saves a widow and her handicapped son from certain financial ruin, and Hope leads a defamed woman back to mental health. The victims were oppressed by the church and rescued by Christian individuals. Indeed, Christianity is a religion of individual, rather than corporate, service in this novel. Dan learns that he can live by Christian principles only by leaving the church, and Hope has long known that true religion takes place in private rather than in a club. Service is an activity that only individuals can perform.

Nature of Resolution

Strong individuals are needed to conquer the selfishness fostered

Strong individuals are needed to conquer the selfishness fostered by institutions in order to engender social harmony. Selfishness is evil because it leads to community disharmony. Selfish individuals usurp the rights of others to become self-actualized, self-sufficient, or self-respecting. Social harmony does not imply community in the organic sense of the term; rather, social harmony in these novels suggests individuals cooperating to ensure their self-determination. Community is little more than a requirement for individual autonomy.

In His Steps envisions Christian community at different levels. The grandest is a world church united by individuals around the globe committed to their pledge of always doing as Jesus would do. The pledge would also promote understanding and cooperation among employers and employees and among landlords and tenants. On the smallest scale, the pledge would draw men and women together in marriage. Whether in the world church or in a single marriage, individuals find self-fulfillment with the assistance of others. Community in this novel is the best environment for individual discipleship.

Community has a more corporate quality in *Black Rock*. The men must learn self-mastery in order to resist their inclination toward reckless self-gratification, but they cannot do so outside the context of community. The sole purpose of self-mastery is community, for when the miners are out of control, they prolong their separation from their families and endanger the lives of the other miners. Community is also an essential condition for self-mastery. Individual resolve alone cannot give the men the will to resist whiskey; the men also need each other's support. Community cannot be easily separated from individuality in this bestseller.

Harold Bell Wright's two bestsellers have a much different view of community. Individuals do not need community. Indeed, Howitt flees from Chicago for the solitude of the Ozarks to meditate on God's nature. Once restored, however, he helps the entire community of Mutton Hollow. Community in *The Shepherd of the Hills* is less of a necessity than an opportunity for the shepherd's faith. The only essential community is marriage according to the laws of nature. Good communities are small ones, and they are more conglomerates of individual personalities than organic wholes.

Wright repeated this notion in *The Calling of Dan Matthews*. The theme of this novel is ministry as service to others. The community provides the opportunity for Christian service. Dan and Hope help others, but they do so one at a time. They do draw inspiration from each other as well as from a few people in the city, but they eventually abandon the city, suggesting that what community there is is temporary and nonessential. The only essential community is the bond between a man and a woman which leads to marriage. Dan and Hope encourage each other, but minister separately, Dan eventually serving humanity by directing a mining operation and Hope continuing to care for the sick. In Wright's bestsellers, community outside of marriage is only minimally necessary.

Method of Attaining Resolution

In these bestsellers, individuals overcome evil in a variety of ways. The methods range from following a formula to relying upon a more mysterious faith. The element of human resolve is integral to all of them, however. They who wait upon the Lord do not appear in these bestsellers.

In His Steps proposes an explicit moral formula. The principle ingredient is discipleship, which means vowing to ask "What would Jesus do?" before making any decision. Answering the question requires biblical, emotional, and community support. The disciple will search for moral principles in the New Testament, pray for guidance and reassurance, and seek out the advice of others. Christian action will take the form of evangelism or social work, but the disciple will decide exactly how to execute these tasks on the basis of his or her personality and opportunities. Of the four religious bestsellers, *In His Steps* is the closest to being a moral cookbook.

There are two steps to attaining resolution in *Black Rock*, but they are not nearly as mechanical as the moral formula of *In His Steps*. The first is to gain the will to resist evil. Such resolve accompanies faith that God forgives and sustains. Second, an individual who trusts God must locate himself in a supportive community, one that is tolerant and forgiving. This ecumenical community is a refuge from temptation because it is understanding and supportive and because it actively tries to solve social problems.

In community, the miners have the strength to resist the most powerful temptations.

A greater element of mystery is apparent in *The Shepherd of the Hills*. Divine laws are present in nature, but the novel never says how they can be discerned. Instead, it gives only two clues. First, moral and spiritual guidance can be gained only in the wilderness, where God's work is not hidden by human creations as it is in the city. Second, only those determined to learn God's ways, those predisposed to spirituality by biological lineage, can do so. Country dwellers with the right blood line are receptive to nature's tutelage, and only they are capable of conquering evil.

This notion of predisposition toward spirituality is repeated in *The Calling of Dan Matthews*. All of the good characters were apparently born that way, although there is no hint of eugenics in this novel. The good characters have iron resolve, which is particularly clear with Grace, who, left with no means of earning a living, would rather commit suicide than prostitute herself. With the exception of Dan, good characters never make mistakes, but even his error was one of misjudgment rather than bad intent. Evil is resisted by sheer strength of will always present in the virtuous.

Conclusion

The belief system in early twentieth-century religious bestsellers suggests that the middle class worried about the increasingly institutional character of American society. While they placed ultimate responsibility for social ills on the voluntary selfishness of individuals, middle-class Americans believed that an unwholesome environment could corrupt all but the strongest of persons. As unwholesomeness became identified with institutions, even the church, the middle class began to long for a bygone era of frontier wilderness and unspoiled nature, when communities were small and cooperative. Rather than condemning the urban life altogether, however, they chose to believe that strength of character and individual resolve were sufficient to overcome social injustices.

Notes

[1]The Charles M. Sheldon collection is located in the Topeka Public Library, Special Collections and Local History Department, 1515 West Tenth, Topeka, Kansas 66604.

[2]The Charles W. Gordon papers are housed in the Elizabeth Dafoe Library of the University of Manitoba. The contents of the collection, manuscripts and notes, are listed in Karen Grislis and Shauna Sanders, "Register of the Charles William Gordon (Ralph Connor) Collection MSS 12," which is available from the library upon request.

[3]Wright gave a similar, but much more detailed, account of his method of constructing novels when he explained how he wrote *When a Man's a Man* (Kenamore 1918, 538-44).

[4]E.P. Dutton, Inc. possesses some of the files of D. Appleton and Company pertaining to Wright's sales. The Lilly Library at Indiana University owns D. Appleton-Century Co.'s records from 1842 to 1952, which include seven scrapbooks and an author file on Wright.

References

Books

Ahlstrom, Sydney E. 1972. *A Religious History of the American People.* Vol. 2. Garden City, N.Y.: Image.

Barrett, David B., ed. 1982. *World Christian Encyclopedia: A Comparative Study of Churches and Religions in the Modern World, A.D. 1900-2000.* New York: Oxford Univ. Press.

Boller, Paul F., Jr. 1969. *American Thought in Transition: The Impact of Evolutionary Naturalism, 1865-1900.* Chicago: Rand McNally.

Cawelti, John G. 1976. *Adventure, Mystery, and Romance: Formula Stories as Art and Popular Culture.* Chicago: Univ. of Chicago Press.

Clark, Glenn. 1946. *The Man Who Walked In His Steps.* St. Paul: Macalester Park.

Commager, Henry Steele. 1950. *The American Mind: An Interpretation of American Thought and Character Since the 1880's.* New Haven, Conn.: Yale Univ. Press.

Conn, Peter. 1983. *The Divided Mind: Ideology and Imagination in America, 1898-1917.* Cambridge: Cambridge Univ. Press.

Connor, Ralph. 1898. *Black Rock: A Tale of the Selkirks.* New York: Fleming H. Revell.

Crane, Charles D., comp. 1909. *A Charles M. Sheldon Year Book.* Topeka, Kan.: Crane.

Doran, George H. 1952. *Chronicles of Barabbas, 1884-1934: Further Chronicles and Comment, 1952.* New York: Rinehart.

Emery, Edwin. 1972. *The Press and America: An Interpretative History of the Mass Media.* 3rd. ed. Englewood Cliffs, N.J.: Prentice-Hall.

Gordon, Charles W. 1938. *Postscript to Adventure: The Autobiography of Ralph Connor.* New York: Farrar & Rinehart.

Greene, Suzanne Ellery. 1974. *Books for Pleasure: Popular Fiction, 1914-1945.* Bowling Green, Ohio: Bowling Green Univ. Popular Press.

Handy, Robert T., ed. 1966. *The Social Gospel in America: Gladden, Ely, Rauschenbusch.* New York: Oxford Univ. Press.

Hawthorne, Hildegarde. 1923a. *Harold Bell Wright: The Man Behind the Novels.* New York: D. Appleton.

Hudson, Winthrop S. 1973. *Religion in America: An Historical Account of the Development of American Religious Life.* 2d ed. New York: Scribner's.

Knight, Grant C. 1951. *The Critical Period in American Literature*. Chapel Hill: Univ. of North Carolina Press.

———. 1954. *The Strenuous Age in American Fiction*. Chapel Hill: Univ. of North Carolina Press.

Loisy, Alfred. 1903. *The Gospel and the Church*. Trans. Christopher Home. London: Isbister & Co.

McLoughlin, William G., Jr. 1959. *Modern Revivalism: Charles Grandison Finney to Billy Graham*. New York: Ronald Press.

Mott, Frank Luther. 1947. *Golden Multitudes: The Story of Best Sellers in the United States*. New York: Macmillan.

Mowry, George E. 1958. *The Era of Theodore Roosevelt and the Birth of Modern America, 1900-1912*. New York: Harper & Row.

Nelson, John Wiley. 1976. *Your God is Alive and Well and Appearing in Popular Culture*. Philadelphia: Westminster.

Noble, David W. 1970. *The Progressive Mind, 1890-1917*. Chicago: Rand McNally.

Nye, Russel. 1970. *The Unembarrassed Muse: The Popular Arts in America*. New York: Dial.

Overton, Grant. 1923. *American Nights Entertainment*. New York: Appleton, Doran, Doubleday, and Scribner's.

———. 1925. *Portrait of a Publisher and the First Hundred Years of the House of Appleton 1825-1925*. New York: D. Appleton.

Rauschenbusch, Walter. 1912. *Christianizing the Social Order*. New York: Macmillan.

———. 1917. *A Theology for the Social Gospel*. Nashville: Abingdon.

Reynolds, David S. 1981. *Faith in Fiction: The Emergence of Religious Literature in America*. Cambridge, Mass.: Harvard Univ. Press.

Reynolds, Elsbery W. 1916. *Harold Bell Wright: A Biography Intimate and Authoritative*. Chicago: Book Supply.

Sheldon, Charles M. 1897. *In His Steps*. Old Tappan, N.J.: Fleming H. Revell.

———. 1925. *Charles M. Sheldon: His Life Story*. New York: George H. Doran.

———. 1938. *The History of 'In His Steps'*. Topeka, Kansas: By the author.

———. 1942. *Dr. Sheldon's Scrap Book*. New York: Christian Herald.

Smith, James Ward, and A. Leland Jamison, eds. 1961. *Religious Perspectives in American Culture*. Vol. 2. Princeton, N.J.: Princeton Univ. Press.

Spurlock, Pearl. 1936. *Over the Old Ozark Trails in the Shepherd of the Hills Country*. Branson, Mo.: White River Leader.

Stead, William T. 1894. *If Christ Came to Chicago!* Chicago: Laird & Lee.

Steel, Ronald. 1980. *Walter Lippmann and the American Century*. New York: Vintage.

Stowe, Harriet Beecher. 1872. *My Wife and I: or, Harry Henderson's History*. New York: J.B. Ford.

Tebbel, John. 1975. *A History of Book Publishing in the United States*. Vol. 2. *The Expansion of an Industry, 1865-1919*. New York: R.R. Bowker.

———. 1987. *Between Covers: The Rise and Transformation of American Book Publishing*. New York: Oxford Univ. Press.

110   A Social Gospel For Millions

Williams, Blanche Colton. 1927. *Harold Bell Wright: The Inspired Novelist.* New York: D. Appleton.

Wright, Harold Bell. 1903. *That Printer of Udell's: A Story of the Middle West.* New York: A.L. Burt.

———. [1907] 1982. *The Shepherd of the Hills.* Reprint ed. New York: Grosset & Dunlap.

———. 1909. *The Calling of Dan Matthews.* New York: A.L. Burt.

———. 1911. *The Winning of Barbara Worth.* Chicago: Book Supply.

———. 1914. *The Eyes of the World.* Chicago: Book Supply.

———. 1916. *When a Man's a Man.* Chicago: Book Supply.

———. 1927. *God and the Groceryman.* New York: D. Appleton.

———. 1934. *To My Sons.* New York: Harper & Brothers.

———. 1942. *The Man who went Away.* New York: Harper & Brothers.

Articles

Adams, Harris L. 1913. "The Career of 'Ralph Connor.' " *MacLean's Magazine* (April), 109-13.

Allen, Frederick Lewis. 1935. "Best Sellers: 1900-1935—The Trend of Popular Reading Taste Since the Turn of the Century." *The Saturday Review of Literature* (7 December), 3-4, 20, 24, 26.

Baxter, Merry. 1970. "Wright Group Hears Adviser Give Challenge." *Imperial Valley Press* (18 February), 1-3.

"Best-Selling Backlist Books." *Bookstore Journal,* September 1984, 98-105.

Bradley, W.A. 1911. "H.B. Wright's 'The Winning of Barbara Worth.' " *The Bookman* 34 (September), 97-99.

Boyer, Paul S. 1971. "In His Steps: A Reappraisal." *American Quarterly* 23 (Spring), 60-78.

Cawelti, John G. 1985. "With the Benefit of Hindsight: Popular Culture Criticism." *Critical Studies in Mass Communication* 2 (December), 363-79.

Christian News Service. 1975. "The Phenomenon of the Religious Best Seller." *Publishers' Weekly* (14 July), 45-47.

Cooper, Frederic Taber. 1909, " 'The Calling of Dan Matthews.' " *The Bookman* 30 (October), 189-90.

———. 1915. "The Popularity of Harold Bell Wright." *The Bookman* 40 (January), 498-500.

Farrar, John. 1925. "Clean Fiction." *The Independent* (5 December), 637-38, 661.

Ford, Corey. 1925. "When a Rollo Boy's a Rollo Boy or, Virtue Triumphant in Three Weeks." *The Bookman* 62 (November), 254-58.

French, Donald G. 1930, "Who's Who in Canadian Literature: Ralph Connor (Rev. Charles W. Gordon)." *The Canadian Bookman* 12 (April), 77-79.

Gohdes, Clarence. 1954. "Old Books." *Georgia Review* 8 (Fall), 354-56.

Grant, Judith Skelton. 1983. "Charles William Gordon." In *The Oxford Companion to Canadian Literature,* ed. William Toye, 306-308. New York: Oxford Univ. Press.

"Grief in the Ozarks over the Divorce of Harold Bell Wright." *The Literary Digest* (21 August 1920), 57-58.

Haddow, Robert. 1899. "The Rev. Charles W. Gordon ('Ralph Connor')." *Book News* (22), 697-700.

Hart, James D. 1954. "Platitudes of Piety: Religion and the Popular Modern Novel." *American Quarterly* 6 (Winter), 311-22.

Harvey, John. 1953. "The Content Characteristics of Best-Selling Novels." *Public Opinion Quarterly* 17 (Spring), 91-114.

Hawthorne, Hildegarde. 1923b. "The Wright American." In *The Bookman Anthology of Essays (1923)*, Edited by John Farrar, 104-12. New York: George H. Doran.

Hendrickson, James. 1925. "Book People Come True." *The Bookman* 62 (October), 192-93.

Kenamore, Clair. 1918. "A Curiosity in Best-Seller Technique." *The Bookman* 47 (July), 538-44.

Millard, Bailey. 1917. "The Personality of Harold Bell Wright." *The Bookman* 44 (January), 463-69.

Milstead, L.C. 1931. "Harold Bell Wright: Press Agent." *The Bookman* 72 (January), 501-502.

"Novels of the Week." *The Spectator*, 14 January 1899, 58.

Paterson, Beth. 1953. "Ralph Connor and his Million-Dollar Sermons." *MacLean's Magazine* (15 November), 26, 56-60.

Patrick, Arnold. 1925. "Getting into Six Figures: Harold Bell Wright." *The Bookman* 61 (August), 673-77.

Phelps, William Lyon. 1921. "The Why of the Best Seller." *The Bookman* 54 (December), 298-302.

"Ralph Connor." *Book News*, February 1901, 355.

" 'Ralph Connor,' by one who knows him." *The Critic*, October 1900, 299, 310-12.

"Readers and Writers: Illustrated Notes of Authors, Books and the Drama." *The Reader Magazine*, December 1904, 105.

Stewart, Donald Ogden. 1921. "How Love Came to General Grant: In the Manner of Harold Bell Wright." In *A Parody Outline of History*. New York: George H. Doran.

Thompson, J. Lee and John H. Thompson. 1972. "Ralph Connor and the Canadian Identity." *Queen's Quarterly* 79 (Summer), 159-70.

"Three Unconventional Churchmen." *The Christian Century*, 10 November 1937, 1381.

Tutler, A.K. 1924. "Our Modern Artists." *Literary Review* (5 April), 645.

van Benschoten, Virginia. 1968. "Changes in Best Sellers Since World War One." *Journal of Popular Culture* 1 (Spring), 379-88.

Watt, F.W. 1959. "Western Myth: The World of Ralph Connor." *Canadian Literature* 1 (Summer), 26-36.

Wright, Harold Bell. 1924. "Why I did not Die." *The American Magazine* (June), 13-15, 82-90.

112 A Social Gospel For Millions

Unpublished Sources

Briggs, William H. 1933. Letter to Harold Bell Wright. 4 January. Tucson: Univ. of Arizona Library, Special Collections.

Cordova, Hector Leroy. 1967. "The Formation of the Social Gospel of Charles Monroe Sheldon, 1886-1919." M.A. thesis, San Jose State College.

Grislis, Karen and Shauna Saunders. 1980. "Register of the Charles William Gordon (Ralph Connor) Collection MSS 12." Winnipeg, Manitoba: Elizabeth Dafoe Library of the Univ. of Manitoba.

Harris, Elizabeth. n.d. "Harold Bell Wright in Imperial Valley, California." P.O. Box 205, Holtville, CA 92250.

Hillman, Paul M. 1984. Interview with author. Grand Rapids, Michigan, August.

Hiltman, J.W. 1931. Letter to Harold Bell Wright. 11 December. Tucson: Univ. of Arizona Library, Special Collections.

Leclerc, Lionel A. 1962. "Ralph Connor: Canadian Novelist." M.A. thesis, Univ. of Montreal.

Nicholl, Grier. 1964. "The Christian Social Novel in America, 1865-1918." Ph.D. dissertation, Univ. of Minnesota.

Wright, Harold Bell. 1931. Letter to J.W. Hiltman. 10 December. Tucson: Univ. of Arizona Library, Special Collections.

_____. 1933a. Letter to William H. Briggs. 25 January. Tucson: Univ. of Arizona Library, Special Collections.

_____. 1933b. Letter to William H. Briggs. 3 March. Tucson: Univ. of Arizona Library, Special Collections.

_____. 1933c. Letter to William H. Briggs. 4 August. Tucson: Univ. of Arizona Library, Special Collections.

Index